Building Good
in a Changing

Sally Rickwss

Building Good Families in a Changing World

Elisabeth Porter

MELBOURNE UNIVERSITY PRESS
1995

First published 1995

Typeset by Melbourne University Press in 10½ pt Baskerville
Printed in Malaysia by
SRM Production Services Sdn. Bhd. for
Melbourne University Press, Carlton, Victoria 3053

This book is copyright. Apart from any fair dealing for the purposes of private study, research, criticism or review, as permitted under the Copyright Act, no part may be reproduced by any process without written permission. Enquiries should be made to the publisher.

© Elisabeth Joy Porter 1995

National Library of Australia Cataloguing-in-Publication entry

Porter, Elisabeth J.
   Building good families in a changing world.
   Bibliography.
   Includes index.
   ISBN 0 522 84648 3.
   1. Family. 2. Parenting. 3. Child rearing. I. Title.
306.85

Contents

Acknowledgements	*vii*
Introduction: Personal Note	*1*
Explanation	*7*
1 Changing Families	*9*
What is a Family?	*9*
Changes in Families	*12*
Individualism	*13*
What Does it Mean to Call Something Good?	*16*
What is a Good Family?	*24*
2 Being Moral	*28*
Character	*29*
Virtue	*31*
Practical Wisdom	*33*
Family Virtues	*37*
3 Being Yourself	*42*
Autonomous Individuality	*42*
Autonomous Individuality in Good Families	*48*
The Family as a Unit	*51*
Individuality and the Well-Being of Families	*55*
4 Including All	*60*
Inclusiveness	*60*
Flexibility	*64*
Negotiation	*66*
Inclusive, Flexible Negotiation in Good Families	*67*
5 Sticking Together	*71*
Faithfulness	*73*
Loyalty	*76*
Reliability	*78*
Faithfulness, Loyalty, and Reliability in Good Families	*79*

Contents

6 Being Truthful	*83*
Truthfulness	*84*
Honesty	*88*
Trust	*89*
Truthfulness, Honesty, and Trust in Social Contexts	*92*
7 Treating Others Well	*98*
Forgiveness	*99*
Justice	*106*
Mercy	*112*
Forgiveness, Justice, and Mercy as Social Virtues	*115*
8 Caring	*120*
Affectionate Care	*122*
Intimacy	*131*
Caring Communities	*133*
9 Loving Friendship	*137*
Love	*138*
Friendship	*144*
Love and Friendship	*146*
Commitment	*153*
Loving Friendship as a Basis for Social Solidarity	*155*
10 Needing Each Other	*156*
Self–Other Relationships	*158*
Domination, Subordination, and Power	*161*
Mutual Recognition and Empowerment	*166*
Interdependence	*169*
11 Having and Owing	*172*
Individual Rights	*172*
Social Responsibilities	*179*
Moral Obligations	*180*
12 Building Small Democracies	*190*
Why are Good Families Important?	*192*
Connections between Private and Public Life	*194*
Good Families, Good Citizens	*198*
Bibliography	*206*
Index	*209*

Acknowledgements

Sue Manser typed the first draft of this book with her customary efficiency and cheerfulness. Sue Ahluwalia, Bev O'Brien, and Helen O'Grady read an early draft. Their comments and suggestions were appreciated, and most have been incorporated into the text in some way. I have benefited enormously from my lively discussions with Bev on the changing nature of families, and particularly on non-conventional families. Jacky Morris read a late draft with a careful thoroughness. I am extremely grateful for her willingness to read the manuscript in a very short time, for her perceptive ideas, and for her many useful suggestions.

A book on the family seems to warrant mention of my own family. I am grateful to my parents, Harrold and Gwenda Steward, for their encouragement of my writing, and for teaching me some of the groundwork that is necessary to create caring families. My siblings, Ruth, John, Judith, Miriam, and Cil contributed in ways they are probably not aware of, in terms of providing me with many instances to reflect on the nature of 'Good Families'.

During the time of writing, my daughter Shantala and my sons Simon and Luke provided me with a host of fresh challenges that made me assess my parenting practices against my writing on good families. Norman, as always, provides me with the intimate love that makes our partnership so precious. He is a loving husband, a wise father, and a good friend.

I dedicate this book to all who seek to build 'Good Families'.

Introduction: Personal Note

In writing a book on the family it is impossible for me as a writer and you as a reader to distance ourselves from the subject matter. We were all born into a family of some sort. However tenuous our present family connections, a male and a female with families of their own contributed biologically to our creation. Where death, war, social calamities or personal distress mean separation from our genetic family, good societies make provision for a social family through fostering, adoption, orphanages, and refugee programmes. Most of us live in families.

This book is meant to provoke memories of childhood, youth, young adulthood, adulthood, middle age, retirement, old age, and all the transitions in between. I am sure the memories will vary, from pleasure, delight, joy and nostalgia, to pain, hurt, guilt and disappointment. The book is meant to jolt you, to ruffle your sensibilities, and to challenge your current family lives. Part of its aim is to encourage you to place yourself and your relevant family members—your parents, spouse, lovers, children, siblings, step-relations, aunts, uncles, cousins, in-laws, and grandparents—in the picture, weighing up the examples I give with your own experiences. This personal focus will be easier for some of you than for others. Reading the book with our particular backgrounds in mind ensures a very practical focus. I will offer you a broad brush outline, but you are the artist, so paint your own picture. My picture will be different from yours.

Let me introduce myself. I was born in 1955 in Java, Indonesia, the fifth child to my medical practitioner father of Australian-Welsh descent, and my active mother of Australian-German descent. I have two brothers (one deceased) and four sisters. For most of our adult lives we have been spread out on various parts of the globe. In 1974 I married Norman who is Irish. He is my dearest friend. Our relationship invites much cross-cultural enrichment and frustrating movement to and fro, from Adelaide, Australia, to Belfast, Northern Ireland. We have children: Kristi-Joy was born and died in 1976; Shantala was born in 1978; Simon in 1980 and Luke in 1983.

My motivation to write a book like this is basically four-fold. First, my family of origin interests me. Coming from a large family, I have always been fascinated by the intricacies of relationships. I had a happy, warm, secure, simple, and religious upbringing, which was toned with formal constraints, and considerable suppression of passions like anger, vocal disagreement, and spontaneous frivolity. My siblings were unwittingly divided into the three older and the three younger ones. We still talk about each other in the way siblings do, and all communicate with each other in varying degrees.

Secondly, my personal situation requires constant reflection on family matters. The death of my first-born child when I was twenty-one years old leaves a marked impression on me, and makes me more sensitive to the fragile nature of life, and the way each new relationship we form influences personal identity. I have worked full-time for most of my married life, as a teacher trainee, a school teacher of English and Physical Education, an undergraduate/young mother, a postgraduate, a tutor, a research assistant, and as a university lecturer. The complexities of organising a household, paid work, children's needs, and adults' needs means that family concerns take up a daily, major part of my life, needing sensitive adjustment and readjustment. In 1992 I had twenty-one days research overseas. This was my longest break from domesticity for eighteen years.

Thirdly, there are intellectual reasons why the family is an important area to study. The family is a complex social institution, shaping and being shaped by wider social structures. The family is changing, and it is important to interpret and to understand these changes because they are contributing to a breakdown of many traditional social and family ties. Literature is slow to consider what can be done to strengthen new family forms. Also, in teaching university courses on 'The Family', it is interesting to watch students' perceptions of their own family situation change. They become sensitised to the fact that good families really do matter to individual security, and to the creation of healthy communities. While everyone's idea of a good family might differ, the *search for good relationships* is common to all.

Fourthly, there are social, cultural, and moral dilemmas that families need to face. We constantly read in the newspapers, see on the television, hear on the radio, listen to our neighbours gossip, and know from our own experiences that all is not well in many families. There is widespread child abuse of a sexual, physical, and emotional nature. In some cultures, children are being sent out to forced labour, to beg, or are sold into prostitution. There is considerable male violence directed at women. Women too, overwrought with the trials of harsh spouses or single motherhood, poverty, and social isolation, are sometimes physically abusing their children. Divorce is steady. Infidelity is rife. Youth delinquency and disillusionment are difficult for parents, social workers, educationalists, and corrective services to handle. There is abuse of the elderly, with children manipulating their parents' finances, and neglecting their emotional and physical needs. There is a general displacement of parental authority, with children claiming their personal liberty as a rejection of all forms of legitimate authority, and as an individual right, but with minimal parallel development of a responsibility to others. In poorer societies many families struggle with ensuring basic sustenance, education, health, and job prospects. In industrially advanced societies unemployment and a global recession contributes to economic hardship, emotional insecurity, and conflict-ridden relationships. All these family crises occur almost as if they are normal.

What sort of societies accept this situation as inevitable? A failure to question the impact of social change on families, and work toward suggesting possible ways of coping with significant change is a real commentary on society's values. Sometimes society reacts only when it hears of the horror stories which make the headlines in newspapers.

- Granny bashing in the suburbs
- Stepfather on child murder charge
- Gangs terrorise youths

4   Building Good Families

- 10-year-old boys hack 2-year-old to death
- Town mourns family murder-suicide
- Mother muffles baby's breath with pillow
- Incest victim commits incest
- Pregnant to school master

We read these headlines and moral outrage is expressed by individuals close to the people concerned, by the community in general, by churches, welfare groups, pressure groups, and by the government itself. We express our outrage by declaring these acts to be unacceptable, indecent, and immoral. Then, when the outcry dies down, life for most people goes back to 'normal'. The abuse, discord, violence, hurt, and unsatisfactory relations chug on without concerted effort to tackle these moral dilemmas.

Globally there are certain moral issues that are publicly debated, particularly issues of abortion, IVF, surrogacy, genetic engineering, donor transplantation, and euthanasia. While these are issues requiring intensive public and legal debate, they are issues many of us may never have to face. It is easy, then, to leave social morality as the sphere of paid professionals, and of service experts. Yet there are many moral issues that affect us all. Many people have an image of morality as outdated or as restrictive. Rather, as I explain throughout the book, our ideas on morality and our moral practices can be progressive, open, and dynamic. Because moral issues constantly arise in our daily relationships, morality is a lively area of debate and of important choices. In thinking about morality, we think about the priorities that we value. In trying to act morally, we make choices that we consider to be sensible, right, or good.

I want to bring out the connections between *private* and *social* morality, and the way in which moral learning and initiative develops in family life. We cannot simplistically blame families for society's problems, nor society for families' problems. The connections between families and societies are intricate. I specifically want to look at what actually goes on in families. What is taught in families? What are children encouraged to believe in, to value, and to work towards? Is there a partial or a total erosion of shared values in our communities? If so, what is replacing this loss? Do many families strive to be good families? What frustrates their efforts? What is a good family? To answer these questions, I am going to argue in this book that without an account of 'the good' that we share in some sense with other citizens, we have no adequate basis for justifying a claim that currently many families are *not* good families. Finding an acceptable justification is not easy.

There has been a breakdown of the moral consensus, a breakdown that largely parallels advanced secularisation. By this I mean that widespread adherence to religious beliefs and practices once provided clear frameworks for people's understandings of right and wrong, good and bad, acceptable and unacceptable. Questioning of the dogmatic, narrow-minded basis to these understandings is desirable, but a wide rejection of shared beliefs results in the absence of a common language of moral decency, where we no longer agree or disagree on what does or does not contribute to making a humane society. For some people, even the idea of decency has come to be associated with narrow or right-wing perspectives, rather than with everyday moral attitudes and capacities. Words like guilt, shame, remorse, honour, courage, and dignity take minimal part in our everyday language. Consequently, community agreement on morality has become hazy.

To call one family a good family, and to argue that another family is not being a good family, we do not want to resort to blaming individuals. Rather, we want to try to help families to become better families, so we need to work out some shared understandings of what it means to call something 'good'. This is not an easy task, for there are many different world-views. My response is to offer a classical (ancient Greek) philosophical notion of the good and show how it is in our families that we first learn to live out our moral lives in concrete relations as a daughter or as a son, to a particular mother or a father, or to an alternative social parent or welfare institution. Indeed, for many women, the family is the major context for the moral dilemmas they face. Yet we do not often discuss what it means to be a good daughter or son, and to be a good mother or father.

Many media-makers, academics, religious leaders, policy-makers, and feminists spend a lot of time criticising the family. There is not enough attention given to working out what really makes 'Good Families'. I believe that there are special moral relationships that emerge in families, relationships that explain the uniqueness of good family life. That is, *special ties like child–parent, sister–brother, uncle–niece, grandmother–granddaughter, and father–son* have *moral weight.* By this I mean that there are unique joys and tensions, social expectations and responsibilities that are attached to these relationships.

For example, a child who is disrespectful to a good parent should feel shame, because respect for those in legitimate authority is fitting. A sister who does not take in her homeless brother may not be acknowledging that one day she may need him to do similarly for her, that reciprocity is a reasonable family expectation. An uncle who does not know that his niece died of an overdose has clearly lost communication with his brother or sister. A grandmother who loses touch with her granddaughter because of some dislike for her outlandish dress breaks an important tradition for the young generation, depriving the girl of continuity with familial heritage. A father who neglects his son and is deliberately cruel to him should feel moral shame, for parenting requires careful, kind attention to vulnerable dependants. Social consequences emerge from not acknowledging the full moral weight of these special ties. In particular, when we diminish the specialness of the ties, we undermine the potential strength of family life to act as a secure framework of connectedness to others from which individuals can face the alienating, isolating rootlessness of much of our modern lives.

I hope this book will offer you some concrete suggestions about what makes 'Good Families'. Approach this book not as an observer looking on, but as a moral agent, as someone who has experience and knowledge of the moral problems in question. You are the artist, so take up your brush. The pictures we paint will differ, but the objects we focus on have similarities. This focus extends the philosopher-novelist Iris Murdoch's view, that *morality* has everything to do with *the way we respond to others,* what she calls our 'loving attention' to particular individuals. In Murdoch's writings moral activity occurs mainly in personal relationships. The moral task is not just a matter of finding ethical principles, or rules, but of making sure we attend to the reality of others. My argument is that the place where we should learn this loving attention to others, this practical morality, is in the family. So, thrust your own family narrative into the forefront of your mind as you read on.

Explanation

Some readers may be thinking that my discussion of good families is quite unrealistic, totally romantic, and too idealistic to be true. Some readers will have experienced major family hurt, violence, pain, abuse, suffering, and grief. Others will come from privileged family backgrounds. In my family we argue, disagree vehemently, hurt each other, fail to be sensitive, bicker, let our emotions boil over, and cry, probably just as your family does. But the picture I paint is *idealistic*, it is something *to aim towards*. It is also a normative picture of the family, which means it is something we *ought* to aim towards. As we shall see, we may share the aim of creating good families, but we differ in how we go about it. This book aims to suggest some guide-lines to help you to decide what your family might work towards.

Three basic arguments weave through each chapter.

First, *good families are important*. Fostering the family's well-being is important to the positive morale and moral growth of individuals within families, to particular family units, and to society in general. Such moral growth means that people are able to connect with each other in relations of trust and care.

Secondly, *our private and public lives are intertwined*. What we believe and what we do in our private lives influences our values and activities in the public sphere, and vice versa.

Thirdly, *good families encourage good citizenship*. In exploring what it means to create good families, we also are providing a basis to outline some of the requirements for good citizenship. This outline is important, particularly in social climates where many of our public figures are corrupt, exploitative, egoists, where individual self-interest dominates, and where economic policies prize efficiency and procedures over the treatment of people, equity, and justice. Citizenship involves a sense of belonging to a community, the opportunity to participate in its activities, and to develop a strong sense of moral obligation to other citizens. This sense of mutual commitment is the underpinning for social interdependence, where we all recognise our need for others, and strive to be of use to others. Moral values and a sense of mutual moral obligation are learned initially in the family. In strengthening families, we strengthen social citizenship.

The first two chapters explore what it means to call a family 'good', and what 'being moral' means. My format in the next nine chapters is simple. First, I explain what is meant by particular family virtues. Secondly, I relate these virtues to the above three arguments that: *good families are important; our private and public lives are interrelated; good families foster good citizenship*. Thirdly, I provide practical examples from everyday life to help explain the virtues and the arguments. The last chapter links good families and good citizens.

The aims of the book are many: to explain some of the major sociological changes influencing families; to draw out the links between family values and social practices; to offer some practical suggestions (and to debate their merits or problems) for improving families that should be shared with partners, friends, relatives, or small groups; to develop some ethical codes for creating good families.

1

Changing Families

What is a Family?

Before answering the question 'what is a good family?' we need to ask and answer two prior questions.
1. What is a family?
2. What does it mean to aim for the good?

Answering the question 'what is a family?' is no longer a straightforward matter. We can define kinship ties clearly; these are blood relationships, so primary kin are our biological parents, their offspring, and our own offspring. The root of most kin relationships has been the nuclear family—a man and a woman, usually married, and their offspring, or a polygamous variant where a man has several wives, or an extended family where several related families live together. There is a natural, biological rationale for the family, namely the desire for physical protection and procreation, but we desire familial intimacy for reasons other than the biological.

As Emile Durkheim, the sociologist, points out, the uniqueness of social units like the family lies in its cultural character. Even physical markers like semen, blood, menstruation, and lactation acquire different meanings in different cultures. For example, biology can detail the physiological explanations of menstruation, but not the cultural—whether a menstrual woman can have sex, mix with men, fly a plane, do surgery, or offer religious sacraments and rituals. These are all issues of cultural contention. Sexuality and family life are part of our cultural construction of meaning. To understand the present context of families is to acknowledge rapid social and cultural change right across the globe.

In the western world in particular, changes are occurring in sexual socialisation in terms of objects of sexual passion, legitimate sexual relations, age of marriage, variations on sexuality, and marital intercourse. Courting behaviour is changing with the transmission of sexual knowledge occurring at younger ages, peer pressures to be sexually active, and fewer prohibitions to permissible relations. Religion still takes an active view on sexuality, marriage, procreation, contraception, extramarital sex, abortion, divorce, and homosexuality. The law provides a framework for family relations in terms of the age of consent, the minimum age of marriage, status of de facto relations, divorce, division of property after a separation, abortion, surrogacy, custody, child support, alimony, illegitimacy, fostering, adoption, guardianship, parental rights and obligations, same sex partners, and family violence. Frequently, the state, law, church, and the family are finely intermeshed with varying tensions, such as when a young rape victim is forbidden by Catholic state legislation to have an abortion. The cultural context makes a significant difference to the degree of tensions.

Furthermore, there are other features that define a family beside blood, law, and procreation. Those people who have lived with us either for a long time, or during traumatic or significant stages of our lives, share family-type bonds—there is a kindred spirit. A common residence is a feature of most families, but of course this changes with marriage, separation, divorce, remarriage, adoption, fostering, or job location. Residency and family are linked. In many cultures, the argument is simple—if close family live together, then those who live together are close family. In some cultures, these significant others are given a family name like mother-sister, or father-brother. Homeless persons who are alienated from blood or legal family often call their 'street mates' their 'family' because of the street codes of protection and familiarity where they share a tunnel, a bridge canopy, a park bench, or leftover food.

Family concepts and policies must be flexible if they are to incorporate the range of relationships and realignments which accompany the re-formations of the family today. Indeed, the family appears in diverse forms. These include:

childless couples; blood ties as with parents, siblings and children; legal ties as with a spouse, adopted children, and step-relations; similar ties that have the same familial features of legal ties, bar the legality, like de facto relations, gay or lesbian partnerships, long-term foster children, and indigenous customary marriages. As Rebecca Bailey-Harris, Law professor, maintains, while law has not fully taken into account all diverse family forms, it needs to, not to undermine marriage or traditional families, but to provide legal security for the various family forms we now have.

It is not my intention in this book to explore the adequacy of these wide-ranging family forms, nor to query their appropriateness. They exist. Rather than comparing or even judging these new family forms, my emphasis is on assessing the *quality of relationships*, and in encouraging the growth of 'good families' of whatever kind. Families are not static. Their structural components vary to include families that are nuclear, single parent, foster, ageing, same sex, extended, or based on a compound or tribe, but they share three main strands: economic, cultural, relational.

1 Economic

The family is an economic construct, a way of ensuring that family members' material needs of food, clothing, and shelter are met. In the west, there has been a change in families from being a productive unit to a consumption unit. Instead of all families participating in productive labour like hunting or fishing, collecting firewood, growing vegetables, tending small animals, baking, and making clothes, we tend to buy most goods. Once basic needs are met, excess materialism often takes over. When the economic structure of 'developing' nations becomes increasingly capitalist, the possession of material goods preoccupies more family units. Further global changes include managing the household economy, deciding on distribution, and questioning a rigid gender division of labour.

2 Cultural

The family is a cultural construct, reproducing traditional, social, religious, political, and cultural values. These values emerge through celebrations, routines, language, rituals, and family traditions, and by participation in broader cultural interactions. Cultural avenues include education, religious institutions, cultural festivals, crafts, art, dance, music, film, drama, and libraries.

3 Relational

The family is a set of relationships that represent a unique way of living together. Families aim to meet emotional needs through interaction with others, providing basic groundwork for patterns of socialisation, skills of decision-making, techniques for handling conflict, disagreements, and crises, as well as for intimacy, security, and a sense of belonging.

Changes in Families

I have deliberately offered a very inclusive understanding of the family. Increasingly, literature from National Institutes of Family Studies and the United Nations adopts a very broad definition of the family as any combination of adults *bound by ties* of consent, birth, adoption or place, who *assume responsibilities* for the above three functions of *economic* physical maintenance, of *cultural* socialisation of any children, and of affective *nurturance*. This means that those who have defined themselves as 'family', but who fall outside conventional understandings of family, must take personal responsibility for ensuring that these three traditional family tasks are fulfilled. What each type of family shares is a commitment to care, a unique sense of belonging, and a degree of intimacy. When it fails to fulfil these purposes, it ceases to function as a family in anything other than a minimal sense.

We frequently hear talk of the breakdown of the family. This is not what is happening. What is certainly true is that the family is changing. The old nuclear family with breadwinning disciplinarian dad, housewife nurturing mum, and a few children, no longer represents the norm in modern western societies. Beside the old nuclear family, there are nuclear families that are not traditional in that they do not adopt a strict gender division of labour, or stereotypical traits. There are now many variations of the nuclear family, particularly with families blended from previous marriages, and many alternatives to it, but the family as a social institution is not being attacked. The criticism is of stereotypical versions of the family based on a strict sexual division of labour, with a dad earning money, doing household maintenance, disciplining the children and controlling his wife, and a mum doing all domestic tasks, nurturing the children, the disabled, men, sick and ageing parents, and being in a subservient position in the family.

We now have an increasing social acceptance of multiple forms of families as defined above. Within these families there are many discernible social trends, which are more evident in the west than in other nations. People are marrying later in life, if at all, and often after having lived together for some time. Women are delaying having children until they have completed study, travelled, are established in careers, or have their house mortgage partially secure. They are having fewer children, and expect their partners to participate actively in parenting responsibilities. Women are entering the workforce in large numbers, in full-time and part-time capacities. The rigidity of the sexual division of labour is crumbling, albeit very slowly. Men's assumed cultural authority is being challenged, as is women's assumed natural subordination. Generally, men's family lives are not changing as quickly as women's lives, but significant changes include men's more visible presence in child-rearing and their questioning of orthodox masculinity. The family is accommodating itself to changing desires and demands of late-twentieth-century society, particularly that of individual self-fulfilment and material comfort.

Individualism

Changing family practices reflect changing social, cultural, and moral values. Often social commentators look at how families are changing, and describe these changes, but do not ask why families are changing, or what the changes are a response to. I suggest that the most significant change within families over the last three decades is a change from shared community values to an absorption of the cultural emphasis on *individualism*. I am defining individualism as an egocentrism where an individual regards most aspects of life only in relation to him/herself. Individualism ranks self-interest and self-preference as the highest priorities. A self-centred individual does not always ignore others, but dumps the concerns of others and the obligations we have to others on to someone else.

It is true that an emphasis on the individual has led to positive changes in the family. For example, we hear a lot of talk about personal fulfilment, self-development, and individual rights. Thinking about these issues and acting on them contributes greatly to individuals' refusal to accept what does not suit or please them, or what jeopardises their basic rights. Many women have the courage to assert their rights to an independent life and finances, no longer to tolerate sexual harassment or control, to create a personally meaningful existence, and to leave the men who undermine their integrity. Men have some of the pressures of sole breadwinning removed, the encouragement to participate in the rearing of their children, and to grow through their emotional expressivity and nurture. Children too are given opportunities to be confident of their right to self-direction, and for their innocence and vulnerability to be protected. These are all positive dimensions to a stress on self-fulfilment and the growth of the individual.

But individualism usually refers to an egocentric independence, a selfish concern for one's self-interest, not just to individuality as an expression of unique identity. Individualism is responsible for many negative effects on the family, especially when it dominates family mechanisms. Self-interest can lead, for example, to all individual family members wanting to be the driver, a real conflict in a one-car family. Clearly, there are times when certain individuals will legitimately demand priority time—during sickness, exams, transitions to school or new jobs, birthdays, or personal disappointments. But when all individuals are continually vying for attention, not only does chaos reign, but the needs of the smaller, more

1 Changing Families 15

accommodating, less vocal, and less powerful are suppressed. Individualism can contribute to such selfishness that people do not even see the needs of others around them.

Individualism destroys broader family networks. Without wanting to grope back to a romantic nostalgia of the 'good old days', it is true that our parents' and grandparents' generations were more oriented to ideals of sustaining groups, whether these were extended families, neighbourhoods, communities, or parishes. The picnics, barn dances, support for the corner shop, and Sunday roasts were all attempts to consolidate group activities, and to place families within clearly defined social groupings. Instead of this orientation, many of us have grown up in several areas, and move our children from suburb to suburb, or even from country to country. Also, we often live far away from our family of origin. People now often pride themselves on being able to choose their friends, rather than be obliged to their families. What this valuation of personal choice leads to is a loosened commitment to the wider extended family. With this loosening comes the related loss of social ties, isolation within suburbia and dehumanising housing estates, and a diminished solidarity with those living in close proximity.

By failing to take seriously the value of human relationships, individualism also undermines any strong sense of moral obligation to others. It enforces the idea that looking after one's self and one's primary family takes precedence over any obligation to be responsive to the needs of ageing, boring, or sick relatives, let alone the crippled man next door, the lonely demented woman at the end of the cul-de-sac, or the strangers lining up for the soup queues. It is important for us to care; looking after our selves is crucial, but only when we recognise the significance of those around us as well.

In summary, families are changing, both in their values and in their practices. Families take many forms. They have a commitment to care, to instil a sense of belonging, and to impart unique forms of intimacy and affection to others. Individualist tendencies destroy much of this commitment and prevent families from acting as a social cement, no longer giving a concrete base to family members, and no longer acting as cohesive social units that help to sustain social bonds.

What Does it Mean to Call Something Good?

Before we explore what a good family might be, we need to clarify what is meant by the term 'good'. We often use the word lightly. I had a good day. He's been a good boy. It was a good movie. It was a good price for a quality jacket. She's got a good body. What all these things have in common is a desirable quality. Good things are good, we desire them because they make us happy. But is this definition enough? Do we understand their desirability in similar ways? If you think a book is good, does it mean that I will agree? Do I necessarily know what you mean by calling it good? Not always. We could disagree vehemently over that. Indeed the disagreement could even impair our relationship if we were arguing over something more significant than a book, like a good house to buy, a good job to move to, or a good time to have children. So we need some consensus on what it means to talk of the 'good'.

To begin this discussion, I want to outline a classical Greek understanding of the good, for two basic reasons. First, my concern is not just with what is morally permissible, for 'morality' as I am explaining it, concerns far more than a set of rules or an externally imposed rigid order. Morality involves more than custom and habit, convention and usual expectations, utility and pleasure, law and set rules. Instead, my concern with morality is in terms of what is morally good. By this I mean that the central question I ask in this book is not 'what should I do?' but *what sort of person should I be*? I explain later that in answering this central question, we will discover what we should do. An emphasis on *being* rather than *doing* tries to understand the actual inner self, the character traits that prompt us to act in certain ways, rather than invoking strict inflexible codes of behaviour. My emphasis is on encouraging active moral agency.

Secondly, it is a concept of the good placed within a broad integrated context, where *the individual's good and the community's good overlap*. So to be a good individual is likely to mean that you are a good family member, a good worker, a good friend, and a good citizen. I want to explore what it means to *be good*, why the *pursuit of the good* is important, and thus why talk of a 'good family' is very meaningful.

Specific virtues

This Greek understanding draws on Aristotle (384–322 BC) and his writings on ethics. In ethics, goodness has two main senses. First, there is moral goodness, or the sorts of *virtues* that make us good persons. Aristotle looks at twelve main ones—courage, temperance, liberality, magnificence, pride, ambition, good temper, friendliness, truthfulness, ready wit, shame, and justice. Hence, in more familiar terms, a person who is confident, self-disciplined, generous, appreciates the good things in life, is proud, is ambitious, is good-natured, friendly, honest, witty, sensitive, and fair, is being good. This person is exercising his or her full capacities and being all that a person can be. In the next chapter I talk about how virtues develop through good character traits, and in the subsequent chapters I expand on those aspects of life most likely to encourage some of the virtues I think to be appropriate for good families today. The following is a list of these virtues, prefaced by the chapter headings as a simplification.

- Being Yourself, *Autonomous Individuality*
- Including All, *Inclusiveness, Flexibility, Negotiation*
- Sticking Together, *Faithfulness, Loyalty, Reliability*
- Being Truthful, *Truthfulness, Honesty, Trust*
- Treating Others Well, *Forgiveness, Justice, Mercy*
- Caring, *Affectionate Care, Intimacy*
- Loving Friendship, *Love, Friendship*
- Needing Each Other, *Interdependence*
- Having and Owing, *Moral Obligations*

Specific purposes

The second sense of goodness is called a teleological goodness. This means that all activities aim at some good, so that *to discover the good* we need *to reveal the purpose* of whatever we are examining. This is not as confusing as it sounds. The purpose of a knife is to cut, so the goodness of a knife is its sharpness. A violin aims to make beautiful music, so a good violin produces quality music. If we apply this idea of goodness to families, then families should aim at some good, and it is a major purpose of this book to work out what is the good that families should be aiming to develop. Goodness involves *specific virtues* and *specific purposes*.

Ethics and good conduct

This classical approach to ethics is quite different from modern approaches. If you interview people in the street and ask them, 'what does it mean to be good?' they may well answer, 'doing what's right'. If you say to a child, 'you've been a naughty little girl', she may whimper, 'but I didn't know I wasn't allowed to do it'. Most people associate 'being good' with doing what we are permitted to do, what we are told to do, or what social mores teach us is right. Also, many modern views suggest that whatever we choose to think is right, is right enough. Now it is not that knowing right and wrong can be removed from ethics, or that independent judgement takes no place; to the contrary, knowledge and judgement are crucial parts of our rules and practices of conduct. Rather, this form of ethics accepts that we cannot know what is right before we know what is good, because a knowledge of the good helps us to understand how to develop good character traits.

Take the cross-cultural taboo of incest—we know this is wrong, not 'just because', or 'because I don't like it', or even 'because it seems wrong', but because the protection of innocent, vulnerable dependants is good, and because unfavourable recessive genes may become dominant. We know that paying back debts, even small amounts, in families is right, because trust is an important basis for relationships. It is good. But if there is a gift given, it is wrong to talk of this as a debt, for a gift given freely in generosity is also good. We know what is right in the context of what is good. Indeed, knowledge of the good enables us to judge whether something is right or wrong.

Our main focus should be goodness, and right action is then a product of our attention to the good. By *goodness* I refer to the excellence of *moral character*, for it is through our feelings, our actions, and our judgements that we express our morality, or the sort of person we are. *Being moral* is essential to living a fulfilled life. That is, it enables us to develop our specific potential. Because we are different, the nature of the good acts that help us to realise our potential may differ. Good conduct extends beyond self-interest to our relationships with others. |As persons of character, and of moral substance, we make moral decisions carefully, considering our options, and being accountable for our choices| Ethics then becomes a series of *suggestions about good conduct*, and how we might achieve this.

Sometimes we may need to accept partial views for partial contexts, for a definitive theory of the good is impossible. Life is too complex for us to declare dogmatically that we know what is good and right for everyone, in every cultural context, in every moral dilemma.|Indeed, a basic part of being active moral agents is in forming a conception of the good, and in selecting action that might realise some good| This approach removes the rigidity and cultural bias of positions that assume their ethics apply in every situation, in every circumstance, in every culture, and in every historical era, in exactly the same way. It puts emphasis on the *agents as moral practitioners* of discernment. As moral agents we actively strive towards deciding what seem to be good decisions.

This does not mean that there are no ethics that we call universal, or that are applicable to all, but it does mean that we should be careful when we invoke such abstractions as 'natural law', as if ethics emerge naturally. Suggestions about the good arise in social contexts. Something like courage is valued everywhere as part of good conduct, but it might involve hunting wild game in one culture, boldly resisting the status quo elsewhere, or it might be particularly relevant to those who have severe disabilities. Honour means a variety of things, from being a soldier or a warrior, to living a life worthy of public praise, fame and noble rank, to a woman's chastity. Given this historical and cultural variance, where notions of the good are open to debate, our understanding of what it means to call something 'good' can go in one of two ways—a toleration of all diversity, or a framework for commonality.

1 A toleration of all diversity

First, in a pluralist society where there are many different world-views, toleration for a range of conceptions of the good is important, permitting widespread diversity of views. Yet this does not mean we have to be neutral regarding the good as if we are an impartial umpire. Claims to neutrality state that there is no widespread acceptance of ways to adjudicate among conflicting views, so one view is as good as another. In cultures that prize tolerance, the teaching of values is complicated. What values, lifestyles, and family practices can we tolerate, and what can we not tolerate? How do we decide this? As Allan Bloom, the cultural critic, argues, clearly an unprincipled tolerance of moral diversity is intolerable. That is, we should not tolerate everything just to prove how tolerant we are. For example, child abuse, the feminisation of poverty, and youth homelessness should not be tolerated. We need to defend *universal human rights* like the right to feel safe in one's own home, the right to an adequate standard of living, and the right to shelter. An overvaluation of tolerance leads to a climate of moral relativism, where everything passes as possible. This breeds moral apathy where we become indifferent to what is tolerated.

A toleration of all diversity also means that there are only minimal common conceptions of the good, so there is no 'ethical glue' holding society together. There is no consensus or commitment to working out what is good for society. At least our grandparents' generation usually taught our parents that lying, cheating, and stealing do not contribute to the common good, and that working hard, doing one's best, and helping others is good. Many of today's parents continue to teach their children similar things, but the motives for doing so are not always as communally inclined, because there is more variance in society's beliefs about what our children should know and do.

My point is that we need a *politics of the common good* not to enforce uniformity, but to allow for a type of diversity where particular forms of individuality are declared worthy of admiration (rather than bigoted, intolerant, dogmatic, and totalitarian forms of individuality), and where the collective forms of the common good that are declared worthy (rather than exploitation, injustice, inequality, and the suppression of right), actually do emerge in common understanding and in law.

2 A minimal ethical code as a framework for commonality

A second possible way to understand the good accepts the importance of cultural diversity, but sees the need to formulate some common ground without which citizens cannot flourish with difference and in unity. I want to argue for a *minimal ethical code* which is valid for all cultural communities, is rooted in the actual things cultures share, and which allows for cultural variations. This code blends *unity* and *difference*, *commonality* and *diversity*. There are basic human needs and functions that we all share. Indeed the anthropologist George Murdock cites cultural universals of:

> art, athletic sports, bodily adornment, cooking, co-operative labour, courtship, dancing, dream interpretation, family, feasting, folklore, food taboos, funeral ceremonies, games, gift giving, incest taboos, laws, medicine, myths, numerals, personal names, property rights, religion, sexual restrictions, tool making.

We all engage in these universals, but in culturally different ways.

As Martha Nussbaum, a quality-of-life theorist, argues, all cultures tell stories to make sense of the unique ways we reveal our humanness. As humans we are born, we live, we die. We are mortal beings who have bodily demands, capacities for pleasure, pain and emotional sensitivities, capabilities of thought, imagination and reason. We socialise, crave intimacy, laugh, work, have connections with nature, and interrelate with others as interdependent beings. We draw on logic and reason in order to discuss. We express a wide range of emotions. We search for symbolic meaning in art, ritual, and nature. We attach religious or spiritual significance to certain objects, beliefs, and festivities. All communities share ways to deal with moral questions like betrayal, or tendencies toward cruelty and deception, but the ways differ. We all play, relate to others, have families, mourn, and celebrate, but we play differently, relate differently, have different family arrangements, different mourning processes, and different ways to celebrate.

Our *differences* build on our *common humanity*. A minimal ethical code accepts rich cultural diversity and suggests that anything is possible in so far as it *affirms human dignity*. Respect for all persons centres this notion of the common good. A minimal ethical code permits a valid basis for intervention by outside organisations like Amnesty International, United Nations, or Human Rights organisations into local practices that undermines this basic respect, like female genital mutilation, the sale of children for prostitution, the persecution of social outcasts, domestic violence, or the sale of persons' bodily parts to be used as involuntary transplant donors.

Contextualised good

What I am suggesting is that we need an antidote to 'thin' notions of the good which basically provide an abstract skeleton of formal, so-called impartial notions of the good, allowing citizens to fill in the body of the skeleton, and to choose their preferred notion of the good. A 'thick' notion of the good acknowledges that the good is not just given in abstract form, plucked randomly out of the sky, but *has substantive content, is socially situated* and *affirms human dignity*. Because ideas of the good which frame our conduct emerge through shared experiences, communal meanings, and historical traditions, we need to constantly question our ideas. For example, historically, societies believed that slaves were useful, and that blacks made 'good slaves'. We now reject this notion of 'the good' as being a distortion of the truth, and a denial of human dignity.

Certainly within cultural traditions there will be conflicts of interest amongst us, even over what constitutes 'dignity', but we can strive for solutions that respect our commonality and our diversity. This *contextualised good* is quite different from merely stating that what is good is what I choose to assert. On this logic there can be no claim to moral superiority, for one assertion is as good as another. On this ground I cannot even criticise your belief in torture of political prisoners, or that men can beat their women partners.

As moral philosopher Virginia Held expresses it, 'morality which ought to guide us in all contexts, ought to guide us differently in different contexts'. Rather than being a set of abstractions or rigid rules, morality is located quite definitely in the concrete situations of everyday life—how we relate to family, friends, colleagues, neighbours, acquaintances, and strangers. So morality is dynamic, it changes with different people with different experiences, and it is often fluid, a medium through which we try to make sense of the experiences in which we participate.

A 'thick' concept of the good respects persons, and cultural traditions, and provides us with the minimal ethical code I am advocating. This code acts as a guide, a road map of possible highways, lanes, streets, paths, and walk-ways to take. It requires adaptation and personal judgement. Travellers on the same tour see it as an adventure, consider the possibilities, talk about options, reflect on consequences, and then choose, being accountable for every little meander they take. I want to demonstrate in this book how it is in the intimate sphere surrounded by those we know well and generally care for, that we ought to learn the art of truly understanding our shared morality, and the moral positions of others.

Coming to this understanding is difficult, for there is a certain mysteriousness attached to ideas of goodness and to ideals of good conduct. We can never fully define goodness because of the enormous range of human possibilities, cultural variations, and human frailty, where no one can be good all the time, no matter what the intentions. Furthermore, given the often contradictory pull and tug of social pressures, we have to anticipate frequent uncertainties, hesitations, bewilderment, trial and error, and less than perfect moral decisions. Moreover, to be less than perfect is not to be wrong, evil, or sinful—it is to *be human*. It is also true that the more we intend to act with regard to the good, the more practice we gain in becoming good, but more of that in the next chapter.

Thus when I describe someone as a good person, I mean that they strive to fulfil the virtues that are characteristic of living an ethical life. Our understanding of what is involved in these virtues differs because ethics, or suggestions about good conduct, develop differently in social and cultural contexts. Therefore I am developing a *minimal ethical code* of good families which affirms our *dignity as persons*, highlights the ethical dimensions of life that we *share with others*, and appreciates how our practical moral lives *differ from others*.

What is a Good Family?

A good family strives to be good for two main reasons—it contributes to creating good social citizens, and it develops special relationships that are unique to families, and which are important for individual development and for well-being.

Social reasons for good families

First, there are external reasons why it is important to maintain good families. The family unit is central to society. Whether the unit consists of a sole parent and a baby, a nuclear family, a large extended family, a polygamous unit, or other family combinations, it is within the family structure that early socialisation takes place. This involves learning language, hygiene, basic education, cultural customs, rituals, social prohibitions, eating habits, and values, in other words, the basic activities of humans.

All these learning processes develop an individual's social dimensions. We are individual social beings, so socialisation aims at the good of social life. Individual personality is forged within the family unit where social behaviour is constructed and social mores are transmitted and interpreted. As Alasdair MacIntyre, moral philosopher, expresses it, we approach our own life circumstances as bearers of particular social identities, as sons or as daughters whose individuality emerges within historical, religious, and cultural traditions. No matter how much we despise our family heritage, we can rarely escape it completely, it has contributed to who we are. We can question our family background, but it provides us with our moral starting point. Clearly not all of family life is geared to the good of constructive socialisation. This is why many of us spend much of our adult life fighting repression, rejection, suppression, guilt, hostility, hang-ups, and fear of the unknown or of connections to particular people. We try desperately, and often in anger, to rid ourselves of some of our socially constructed personhood.

Nevertheless, the family unit ideally plays a central positive role in society in providing a sense of security, a retreat, and somewhere to belong. After a busy day at school, at work, being out on the land or travelling, most people like the sense of coming home. This is often the case even for women and children who are victims of abuse within the home, or where the home is very simple with basic living conditions. There is an important value attached to privacy, and to familiarity, that there is a little corner of the world that belongs to me or to you, even if it is just a mat on the floor or a corner of a room. Ordinary objects or places can take on special significance when associated with the home. A teddybear can be homely for a child in hospital, a family photo for the executive in the foreign hotel, the same bus shelter for the vagrant, or a familiar field for the travelling Gypsies. Good families ensure that they fulfil these two external rationales: that they transmit social and cultural understandings of *good social behaviour*, and that they provide a strong sense of *secure belonging*.

Special relationships unique to families

Secondly, there are reasons internal to good families that make such families important. This relates to the fascinating dimension of human uniqueness, that we are simultaneously *individual and social beings*. Indeed, our individuality emerges only in context with others. We are not isolated beings. The presence of others in our lives helps to form our individuality: we are truly *selves-in-relations*. Just as our understanding of ourselves depends in part on our genetic heritage, sex, race, and personality, we also are defined in part by our social heritage, ethnicity, cultural background, and social relationships.

Individual and social factors are intertwined. Not only do we know ourselves in the family in relation to others, that is, as daughter, son, mother, father, sibling, cousin, spouse, aunt, uncle, grandparent, and/or step-relation, but our distinctive personality emerges as a result of these relationships. It is in families that we form and express emerging self-identity, so that we can recognise ourselves as individuals who are members of various community groups—family, education, church, work, social, and civic. As community members, we are thus accountable for the way we express ourselves. As moral agents, our life is a quest for self-understanding of how to make sense of living a good life, and understanding our part in other life stories.

This quest starts in the family. Family relationships are special relationships in several ways. As an angry teenager might retort, 'I didn't choose to be born'. Most family relations, with the exception of one's partner, are involuntary. We cannot choose our parents, our biological children, our cousins, our siblings, or our in-laws. Furthermore, these family relations are not interchangeable. My biological mother will always be my biological mother, even if I gain a stepmother, a foster mother, or if a woman adopts me. Especially when there are bonds of intimacy, no one else can replace the particular person, whoever this may be—an estranged lover, a de facto executive on an overseas assignment, or a relinquishing mother craving her baby adopted a long time ago. It is specific persons we love, need, rely on, and care for, or sometimes despise, neglect, resent, or avoid within families. This makes family relationships quite different from the friends we choose, or the people we work with, and with whom we have formal relationships.

To summarise, good families play an important role in society. They introduce its members to forms of social behaviour that culture deems worthy of pursuing. They foster individual identity and social identity. A good family tries to ensure that physical needs are met. It provides a secure place of belonging, a shelter, not just a roof over the head, but a real emotional canopy from all sorts of storms, a place where we find warm caring, secure togetherness, and a tolerant acceptance. A good family encourages strong assertive identities to whom younger children can relate and test their developing personalities. A good family appreciates each member as important, as necessary to the unit, and affirms each member as part of an interdependent network.

What is learned by being part of an intimate sphere is the need to care for those around us, that we have a personal stake in the well-being of others. For example, men's increased participation in the nurture of small children should develop their caring skills and decrease their propensity to be violent in the home. Strong ties in the intimate sector should increase charitable tendencies in the community. When we have experienced care, and have cared for others, we understand the importance of providing for vulnerable others, especially since one day we too might be ill, disabled, unemployed, very old, or desperate for care.

What we need to explore now is this—if it is true that what is thought to be good depends on the character of the individual in the context of cultural communities, how is this character to be encouraged in the family? If we are getting a clearer picture of what a good family is, what is moral character, how do we build good character, and what qualities allow character to grow?

2

Being Moral

We are striving to understand how to develop the well-being of good families. An important part of this well-being is the development of character in each individual family member. One of Aristotle's most powerful insights is that moral life is based on *ethos*, or the distinctive character that forms within specific social contexts. I am arguing that there are real observable deficiencies in the ways in which modern societies go about developing the character-building capacities of citizens. The prevalent moral *ethos* is lacking in substance. The reasons for the shallowness of character and how this might be rectified needs to be spelt out. In this chapter I make connections between:

- goodness
- moral character
- virtue
- practical wisdom.

There are links between these four aspects of being moral. The links by themselves do not make the chain, it is their combined effect that is important. In each culture what is thought to be *good* depends on the *character* of the individual, and the specific *virtues*, or the way the individual maintains character-building community customs, and thus practises *wisdom*. For example, a school *ethos* might foster team sports in order to cultivate individual traits of persistence and determination, while also valuing the social co-operation of the team endeavour.

Sometimes there is agreement on what should constitute this *ethos*, but as members of cultures, communities, and families, we cannot totally agree on what constitutes the good,

28

so we must look for the possibility of it in people's actions, that is, in actions that appear to be in accordance with virtue. Virtues are dispositions of character which make a person inclined toward the good. Practical wisdom is the demonstrated capacity to act with regard to good habits and good judgements. Let us look in more depth at character, virtue, and wisdom, and see how an understanding of these three dimensions to moral life can strengthen good families and move closer to the desire of Martin Luther King. 'I have a dream. My four little children will one day live in a nation where they will not be judged by the colour of their skin but by the content of their character.'

Character

At a party or social gathering, you might hear the phrase, 'oh he's a real character', meaning a particular man is witty, charismatic, charming, or fun, having a very distinctive personality. He may even be eccentric in a pleasant way. A teenager may be accused of being 'a complete jellyfish, totally spineless, having no character at all', meaning the person is weak or lacking in courage in acting on decisions. Someone might say, 'I like her character', which means they like the attributes, qualities, and temperament of this woman's personality. 'He has character' might single out one distinguishing characteristic, like honour or strength. 'She's got a good character', means she has a good reputation. In the past, character references referred to this repute, just as character assassinations attempt to destroy someone's standing in the community. We call someone a 'shady character' when we are not entirely clear about the sort of person they really are, but we suspect they have many undesirable attributes. A 'character' can be a person in a story, a play, or a film, playing the role of someone with particular dispositions. Indeed, the morality plays of the late fourteenth century dramatised allegories of good and evil fighting for men's and women's souls. The moral strength of the characters was forcibly portrayed. Clearly we use this term 'character' in many different ways.

What exactly is moral character? Certainly it involves the combination of natural and socially acquired features that distinguish one individual from another. Not all these features will be desirable, which is why we do talk of bad character, poor character, weak character. In classical ethics, which is the version of ethics I am drawing on, moral character refers to the overall way an individual lives a life more or less determined by the good. *Moral character* is not a passion or a faculty; it is an *active inclination toward the good.* I explain later how we learn the finer points of what is good, but now we are trying to understand more of what it means to call something 'good'. Either we live a life striving for the good, or we live a life rejecting the good, or we are indifferent and careless, or we are not sure what the good might be, so we muddle along, as a moral drifter.

Given this stress on its active nature, a classical notion of ethics sees the main purpose of education to reproduce in each new generation the moral character suited to the society in question. In my reckoning, education should not be chiefly about preparing children for the computer age, technological advances, information explosions, or even for industry and the workforce in general. Rather, it should be about developing the moral character of students, developing traits of determination, persistence, and diligence; and in the striving towards moral excellence, the skills of numeracy, literacy, sciences, humanities, social sciences, art, craft, music, sport, drama, and technology have a meaningful context. Without this context, the process of learning as a developmental unfolding of potential is pushed aside in the interests of skills required by a technological society. The exercise of good moral character brings us closer to living a full human life.

It is in families where much of this initial introduction to the educative disclosure of each child's capacities, so important to character-building, takes place. As we help a young child rebuild the blocks that keep tumbling, to solve a difficult problem, and to learn new ways of thinking and doing, we are assisting the child's ability to understand hidden aptitudes. When this assistance includes a stress on developing moral character, individuals are encouraged to explore possibilities for a life actively influenced by the good. Because there is no universal agreement about the good, we need to look at what actions strive toward the good, for, as we have already noted, there are many alternatives. Our goal here is to discover how moral character might incline us towards certain good actions, rather than others. To do this, we need to look at actions that are in accordance with virtue.

Virtue

Just as 'character' has many different uses, so does 'virtue'. 'She's kept her virtue' means that she has retained her innocence, her chastity, her virginity. If 'he makes a virtue of necessity' he agrees to do something unpleasant, awkward, or time-consuming, with a good nature, because someone had to change the nappy, unblock the sewerage, change the tyre, or drive the children to and fro. 'There's a real virtue in doing that' means that there is some admirable quality or trait gained by the activity being commented on. Sometimes we refer to a particular virtue, like the virtue of tolerance, where we endure or permit things that we do not necessarily agree with. The cardinal virtues, central virtues adopted by Christianity, are: prudence or caution; justice or fairness; fortitude or strength of mind; temperance or restraint in yielding to desires. The virtues proposed by Christian theologians as a complement to the others are faith, hope, and charity. All religious world-views urge a 'life of virtue', and there are overlaps in the virtues different religious perspectives advocate.

I am using *virtue* in this book in the sense of the *quality and practice of moral excellence*. Excellence refers to goodness, not to any unrealistic, superior, unattainable distinction. Virtue is the disposition of character, it is the capacity that enables us to function well, and it motivates us to respond morally. So the virtues of a good businesswoman refer to her professional skills, not her moral virtues, although of course these are related. The virtue of a woman or of a man is the state of character which makes this woman or man good. If we hear that the businesswoman is a good person, we know this refers to her moral virtue. In business she is honest, trustworthy, and fair.

Aristotle gives a clear account of virtue which is his central moral category. He defines virtue as excellence in fulfilling one's proper task or purpose. The excellence of a knife is its sharpness, with an athlete it is athletic skill. If our final goal is happiness, or *living life well*, then, for Aristotle, happiness is life lived in accordance with virtues, striving towards moral excellence. In a world that defines the good life in terms of material comforts and hedonistic pursuits, this ancient idea of life lived 'morally well' is foreign to many.

Therefore let me explain virtue in more detail. Virtuous actions proceed from choice. They are actions which involve a deliberate desire to fulfil properly our human purposes. This is why an account of the virtues needs this sense of *telos*, or end purpose of human existence, of some good to which the virtues contribute. We have all asked the questions, 'why are we here?' and 'what purpose is there to life?' The answers to these questions are never straightforward. In the previous chapter we noted shared common features of humanity, like reason, emotions, social life, and the search for spiritual and symbolic significance, of which there are numerous cultural and individual adaptations. Virtues are directed towards human fulfilment. Working out this personal direction of how best to develop our potential is not an isolated pursuit, it gains an intelligibility from a community's concrete life, that is, we must be able to see evidence of the virtues, and different virtues may seem appropriate in different contexts, which is our focus for the remaining chapters. Again, it is not that we have to tailor our lives to a set of narrowly preconceived abstractions or dogmas, the emphasis is on our own judgement.

Virtues manifest themselves in different types of situations. Take the virtue of compassion, a disposition that sustains kind, considerate practices. The way we exhibit this kindness differs, and marks us as distinct moral beings. A man can be compassionate in his relationship with his surly father, in his work as a trade unionist facing industrial relations issues of widespread retrenchment, and in his entanglements with a persistent embittered lover from the past. Each of these relationships affects the way he understands compassion. This *contextual nature of virtues* contrasts with modern individualism that says, 'I am what I choose to be', the self detached from social tradition. Instead, historical identity, social identity, moral identity coincide. From a position of partial self-knowledge we move in our varied social positions in quest of how best to exercise the virtues appropriate to our life experiences. The son, the unionist, the ex-lover respond to social situations differently. To know when and how to adapt virtues requires practical wisdom.

Practical Wisdom

Practical wisdom is the evidence of a capacity to act with regard to the good. It involves two things—*good habits* and *good judgements.*

Good habits

First, moral learning is a gradual process whereby we simply learn by doing. None of this happens overnight. We all have the capacity for virtue, but this capacity must be developed as habit through continual practice. We become virtuous by engaging in virtuous activities, but we do not always know what these activities are. The process involves much trial and error. Through education and habit, observation and deduction, reflection and experience, mistakes and sound choices, we come to understand which virtuous actions are right for specific situations. This involves a lifetime of learning. A heavy onus is on parents and teachers to inculcate virtues from early childhood, so they become a kind of second nature, a habit so long practised as to seem innate.

Our ability to act well depends on the quality of our habitual objects of attention, so that we learn to be moral by *being moral.* We become just by doing just actions. We learn to create good families by *being good families.* We learn what is right for good families by focusing on what seems to be good for the family's well-being. These learning processes are never easy, what seems to be good may change, but the more this focus on the good becomes habitual, the more frequently we act with practical wisdom.

Good judgements

Secondly, as well as good habits, practical wisdom requires good judgement. Moral judgement is much more complex than applying straightforward rules. 'You should not steal' is a rule, but in times of war, starvation, and famine, our judgement might result in choosing to steal a loaf of bread. The judgement that comes from good habits requires assessing each particular context and adjusting to circumstances. If moral learning involves learning by doing, the central facilitating resource for improving moral judgement is *experience*. We become better, or more ethical, through experience and practice, which enables us to make finer, sharper, and more sensitive discriminations in all the choices and decisions we must make. This is not to say that wisdom always comes with age, for a young person who has lived through a wide variety of life experiences, or who has thought deeply, may have learnt more than an old person who has been sheltered from a lot of reality, or who has lived an unreflective life. It is to say that the more we have seen of life, the more we *should* develop the capacity to see moral actions in moral terms—as cowardly, generous, mean, ungrateful, principled, dutiful, unjust, trustworthy, wrong, right, bad, or good.

Moral reasoning draws on experience: it requires us to apply our previous knowledge of the good to judge each particular moral dilemma. Having experienced a petty, callous, and selfish relative gives us grounds to say, for example, 'she's so mean to her son'. One way of increasing the experiential basis of learning for children is through stories. Myths, legends, fables, and fiction allow the imagination to watch good and evil, giants and leprechauns, witches and fairies, goblins and pixies, or television's superheroes and evil forces of the universe. These contrasts give children the opportunity to test their powers of moral discrimination, assess the way others live, and observe how good usually triumphs in children's stories.

Good judgements call for discrimination and adaptability of virtues for different circumstances. For example, returning someone's belongings is right in most circumstances, but a similar action in atypical circumstances is wrong. We do not hand a violent man who has lost his temper his axe, knife, or hammer. Telling the truth is a virtue, but many of us lie to protect our best friend's reputation, and most of us would lie to protect the lives of our friends, our children, or our lovers. Wisdom, as the philosopher Philippa Foot puts it, can be contrasted with cleverness. Cleverness is the ability to take right steps to any end, but wisdom relates to knowing what ends are worthy of pursuit. The stockbroker who spends most of his waking time dealing with massive amounts of money might be a clever, wealthy broker, but his goal of becoming a millionaire before he is forty might not be wise. It may contribute to his wife looking for another man who will spend more time with her. The broker might reach his goal, but he may be a lonely, stressed millionaire divorcee in the process. *Wisdom involves good judgements.*

Knowledge, experience, and choice

An emphasis on practical wisdom in the form of good habits and good judgements commits the moral agent to an *active moral state*. It accepts that what constitutes the good must be discerned in actual situations, and knowing what is or is not appropriate calls on a wealth of experience in order to make a good judgement. Knowledge and experience are not morally opposed. We can explain rationally anything we have personal knowledge of. Indeed, having experience of what a tantrum-prone toddler is like in the middle of a shop means that we have an experience base from which we know what response is likely to calm the child. Knowing what it is like to live with a mean spouse often encourages us to be generous. Having to face a loved one's death often makes us more sensitive to the fragility of life. Such a responsiveness calls less on theoretical concepts of knowledge and morality than on a practical awareness of if, where, when, how, to whom, we ought to act in regard to specific issues.

Practical wisdom draws on knowledge, experience, and the acceptance of responsibility for our choices. Individual and social ideas of good practice require a great deal of specific practical reasoning, a real receptiveness to each new context, the people involved, and their social situations. What works in one community may be ineffectual in another. Religious and aid organisations are learning this need to consider indigenous issues. Discussion with those immersed in the local conditions is requisite to making an informed concrete application of moral principles. In all communities, many choices have to be made, but there should be much prior deliberation to mediate between general principles that seem to dictate what ought to be done, and particular situations that seem to need new alternative resolutions. For example, in regional communities that depend on large families for agricultural subsistence, a family planning clinic run by foreigners might upset the locals. Dialogue, information, and training indigenous health workers to appreciate the benefits of health, nutrition, safe sex, and good infant care incorporates more scope for acceptance of this sort of clinic.

Moral judgement requires choosing among morally different alternatives, but it is more than mere choice. It is not just a matter of repeating successful actions; it involves reasoning, reflecting on options, and making creative responses to each new situation. The way we react to our oldest daughter is not necessarily appropriate for our youngest son. We might be trying to maintain an equilibrium of kindness and firm discipline, but practical wisdom requires adaptability.

I argue, along with Lawrence Blum, political theorist, that personal relationships vary according to the type of bond, and the particular people involved: parent–child, grandfather to grandson, aunt to nephew, best friends, oldest friend, ex-lover. These particular relationships affect how we act towards specific persons. Indeed the moral dimension of these relationships is bound with this particularity and the different way we respond to them. Care of our healthy brother involves different considerations from care of our invalid father. Responding to the particularity of relationships is a fundamental dimension of moral life. It requires of us an attempt to know people well, to know how to respond to them. For example, care for our brother might mean responding to the things he likes—folk music, Thai food, and hang gliding, whereas with knowledge of our father, we might show him old slides, play classical music, and listen to his wartime stories.

To understand special relationships is to understand how these people find meaning in their lives, and to react with great attentiveness. This is more important than trying to be morally right according to some strict code that does not permit flexibility, or *contextual application.*

Now we can draw the links between *goodness, moral character, virtue,* and *practical wisdom.* They are intricately connected. The pursuit of the good affirms our human dignity. Moral character involves specific virtues and goals that are worthy of pursuit. Virtues entail skills of the good life, good habits, and good judgement in fulfilling our tasks. Virtues reflect moral character and rely on experience, context, and practical wisdom. Virtues give sense to the notion of a human being of good character, a being with an active inclination to the good. Similarly, vices entail failures in the good life, they undermine moral character and reveal a weakness in practical wisdom. In the following chapters we will explore virtues appropriate to sustaining good families. I am going to outline briefly nine key areas of family life that we will be exploring in depth.

Family Virtues

1 Being yourself, *autonomous individuality*

As moral beings we are autonomous, capable of making individual choices, of being accountable for these choices, and being responsible for their consequences. We share this capacity with others, with whom we express our diverse individuality. It is the role of families to cultivate this autonomous individuality, allowing individuals to be themselves, and to respect the integrity of people's choices, to allow young adults to learn through their mistakes, so long as the learning outweighs the possible harm of the mistake, and to grant household members space to be themselves.

2 Including all, *inclusiveness, flexibility, negotiation*

The family is a social unit. Part of the excellence in fulfilling the family's task as a social unit is to ensure that all members really feel included. This means different things for different individuals, and will vary according to the life cycle. Teenagers, exploring their independence might not want to be included in all family activities, preferring to explore personal identity within their own peer group. Flexibility and negotiation is an essential part of aiming toward the good of inclusive family life. This might involve trade-offs—a teenager goes off to his party on the Friday night and visits his grandparents on the Saturday. The virtues of inclusiveness, flexibility, and negotiation are contributing to the good of the family as a flourishing social unit.

3 Sticking together, *faithfulness, loyalty, reliability*

Those family members disposed to be faithful take seriously the importance of being devoted to other family members. This commitment instils a sense of loyalty, that you protect those to whom you are devoted, you keep coming back to them, and you show your attachment to family members by being dependable. Faithfulness includes sexual fidelity for partners, and loyalty includes support for individual members. Parents watching young Johnny play his first game of soccer do not support the opposition team. Loyalty also includes providing security for the family unit. Reliability is part of this dependability, that the lawns will be mown when there is a promise to do them, the child will be taken to the park when the promise has been made, the teenager will arrive home on the agreed curfew time, and if there are partners, they can be assured of being reliable, loyal, faithful friends.

4 Being truthful, *truthfulness, honesty, trust*

Knowing that our child, our sibling, our parent, our partner is showing us due respect by being truthful is a crucial part of being in a good family. People prone to lying, cheating, and stealing cannot be trusted. They are often honest only when it suits them, and even then you cannot always be sure, thus you hide the chocolate bars, the loose change, the alcohol, or the jewellery, because you cannot trust someone in the household. Good families are open families: they discuss sex, likes, dislikes, disappointments, and joys with an uncomplicated straightness. Genuine relations develop, sincerity is valued, and the family members trust each other with precious moments.

5 Treating others well, *forgiveness, justice, mercy*

We are frail beings; we all make mistakes. Despite aspiring to the good, we hurt others unintentionally, we are not always fair, we get tired and give harsh punishments to our children, or say horrible things to those for whom we really do care. We have regrets in the way we treat other family members and do not always know how to deal with our sadness. Often worse for us is having to suffer the hurt imposed by others, a drunken father, a lying daughter, a stealing son, or a nagging mother. In aspiring towards good families we forgive, we cease to blame people who have done us wrong; we pardon them, we let them off, often even without their saying sorry. This is enormously difficult to do; for some people or in certain situations it is impossible.

In this context, justice is not merely a principle of fairness, or of giving people what they are due, but it is a commitment to set right what has not been right in personal and social relations. Sometimes there is a call for mercy, a special form of compassion. We are being merciful when we assist someone that has no automatic claim to our assistance. It is a gracious act. The ethical factor binding acts of forgiveness, justice, and mercy is the need to treat others well.

6 Caring, *affectionate care, intimacy*

In good families there is ample evidence of affection, intimacy, and care. Tenderness and emotional feelings of sentiment prevail through touch, gestures, pleasantries, verbal encouragement, and visible signs of affection. Good families foster a unique intimacy where familiarity and mutual understanding result in warm personal relationships. Care is evident for there is an intensity of attachment to family members and a delight in family relationships.

7 Loving friends, *love and friendship*

Loving friendship is a virtue that all partners should share, a deep soul companionship, and a virtue that is wonderful when children and parents and siblings also share in it. The latter forms of friendship emerge in contexts where brothers and/or sisters are very well known to each other, they have spent a lot of time with each other, they have been allies in a cause, sometimes against one or both parents, and their friendship is built on familiarity of experience. They might fight like cats and dogs as children, or even ignore each other, but friendships often develop as adults. Friendships in families create unique bonds.

8 Needing each other, *interdependence*

Interdependence acknowledges each family member as important; we depend on different family members for different contributions, but this dependency is mutual. Within good families there is a milieu of reciprocity, a fine balance between giving and taking. There is a mutual recognition of all persons as worthy of respect, and of the way that both individuality and social awareness flourishes through our interdependence. Dependency makes us vulnerable as we acknowledge our need for others, but it is also a unique expression of our humanity. When our dependence on others is balanced by others' dependence on us, there is a rich social and moral valuation given to mutual care.

9 Having and owing, *mutual obligations*

Good families accept that there is a range of duties, specific requirements, promises, particular understandings, and responsibilities that emerge from being a family member. We all have individual rights and it is important that families respect these rights. Individualism allows us to take care of ourselves and hope that someone else will look after others. Yet we have certain obligations to those with whom we are connected, and deep responsibilities to those with whom we are intimately connected. Indeed, a strong sense of moral obligation is a crucial moral underpinning for society itself. Good families create the contexts in which individual rights and social responsibilities are in fine balance.

In the next nine chapters, we examine these virtues in more depth, exploring three key questions.

1. Why are good families important?
2. How do our private and public lives influence each other?
3. How can we create good family members who are good social citizens?

To answer these questions, we need to pursue three further dilemmas.

1. How can good families best encourage moral character?
2. How can virtues contribute to the well-being of good families?
3. What family practices foster the development of practical wisdom?

In the concluding chapter we look at how strengthening families strengthens societies. Good families build the moral character of family members who proceed into their work settings, their community activities, and their social relationships as good persons.

3

Being Yourself

Good families develop *autonomous individuality* in their family members. What does this mean? It means letting family members *know themselves* and *be themselves.* Autonomy is quite simply self-determination, the freedom to determine our own behaviour and actions. Autonomy is a thoroughly modern concept, absent from the ancient ethics I draw on which articulates the social, political, and communal aspects of life. In Chapter 10 we develop the social virtue of interdependence, but it is necessary now to understand the individual virtue of autonomous individuality. When we are autonomous, we act according to our own principles. We assess options and make individual decisions and moral choices.

Our individuality is the distinctive expression of that choice, it distinguishes us from other personalities and affirms the unique character of our identity. Two brothers might choose to drop their girlfriends on the same day. They decide independently of each other and act for different reasons, but their choice is basically the same. One brother does it sensitively, wanting to minimise the hurt to the person he has spent a lot of time with, and he remains friends with the young woman. The other brother is abrasive, harsh, and alienates his friend. The same choice reveals distinct responses. I have raised three children to value their self-determination, but their distinctive expressions of autonomous individuality are quite different.

Autonomous Individuality

To understand why some of these differences occur, we need to trace the emergence of autonomous individuality in the early psychological development of self-identity. As an infant, dependence on others is crucial for physical survival. In order to establish a separate identity and form relationships with others, there has to be a way for infants to realise that they are separate beings, different from the other people who figure in their lives. There has to be some way the young child knows 'this is me', and 'this is you'. The child tests this differentiation by early signs of self-assertion—the dummy being thrown on the floor knowing someone will pick it up, the crying at night to gain attention, or the smiles and gurgles when anyone spends time with the child. All these patterns are early ways of saying, 'I am starting to recognise that I am an independent person, a subject with objective status'.

Gender differences

The development of this autonomous self-identity often has some gendered differences. In the traditional stereotypical upbringing of children, it is usually a woman who acts as the prime carer. In the absence of a father, who often appears for short moments at the start and the end of the day, a male child often revolts against this absence and lack of a masculine role model by defining himself in opposition to the woman caring for him, as someone who is conspicuously different from her. To use a common example, a boy child may react against his mother's gentle, quiet ways by being deliberately boisterous and aggressive. Not only does this type of reaction often instil long-lasting negative attitudes to women in general, but it also fosters a specific self-identity as an independent separation from others. This identity can lead to difficulties in later life with relationships with women, when men define their selfhood as being opposed to their prime carer, their mother. These men do not value women, nor see their identity formation to be positively influenced by people who are significant to them. Tied with these attitudes is men's typical reluctance to express their emotions and to nurture children. Thus the traditional stereotypical upbringing of boys often contributes to an identity devoid of emotional connections.

In contrast, a traditional upbringing of girls typically establishes their sense of self in relation to their prime carer who is also female. Their femininity is usually reinforced in a context of nurturance, affiliation with other females, and an acceptance of emotional expressivity. While girls often have highly developed skills of communication, and value their friendships, their sense of self is often so embedded in their connections to others, that their sense of separate autonomy may be ambiguous.

Imagine the scenario. Kurt is a mechanic. He leaves the house at 7.00 a.m., returns at 7.00 p.m., drinks in the bar on Friday nights, works on friends' cars on Saturday to earn extra money, and plays sport most of Sunday. Jane, his de facto wife, looks after Maria, a five-year-old and Tom a four-year-old. Young Maria has mixed predominantly with women. Her baby sitter, kindergarten and school teachers, and health workers are all women. She realises her identity as a girl through her relationships with these women and appreciates these connections. She maintains her emotional attachment to her mother with her developing sense of individual selfhood. In contrast, Tom does not see much of his same-sex parent; he never has. Kurt plays with him before bed, rough and tumble games that Jane thinks excites Tom. Tom has started bullying Maria, and does not want Jane to cuddle him. What Tom probably is doing is defining himself as not-female, as quite different from his mother and sister who are very affectionate to each other. His sense of separate identity emerges as self-control, as an emotional distancing from those he perceives to be quite different from him.

Initiation rites in many indigenous cultures affirm this practice of separation as formal acknowledgement of male gender identity formation. The purpose of these rites are twofold—young boys are taken from the tribe or village to prove their manhood, and to assert that they are not women. In the west, a father who takes his son, an uncle who takes his nephew, or a grandfather who takes his grandson to a prostitute for his first sexual experience also affirms this rite of autonomous masculinity. Masculinity is here defined as an emotional distance from others.

The assumptions and practices relating to this gender restrictiveness and traditional socialisation pattern are diminishing. Decreasing numbers of children are being raised in two-parent families. Some men in one-parent or in two-parent families are becoming more active in the responsibility of parenting. This comes both as a response to demands women are placing on men in wanting to explore other areas of self-fulfilment in addition to mothering, and it is a response of men not wanting to miss out on the active experience of fathering. Men are increasing their involvement in the physical care of children, transportation, play, leisure, and educational aspects of child-rearing. As men become more open in their emotional expressivity, they are increasingly willing to express their affection to children. In some instances, this increased participation of men offsets women's reduced time spent on nurturing children. Women's activity in the paid workforce means that they are less available to cater exclusively to children's emotional needs. This has its positive and negative side-effects.

On the negative side, women often experience guilt at leaving children in childcare or with relatives. The triple shift of paid labour, domestic labour, and childcare is a demanding physical and emotional burden. On the positive side, women's own sense of autonomy has increased as a result of the opportunity to explore new avenues of self-direction. More women have made it clear that they will not assume sole responsibility for the nurture of others. Remember, too, the structure of the family is changing. Many once married couples, de facto couples, and blended families do not uncritically absorb the traditional roles and values of old forms of nuclear families.

Sole parents, the majority of whom are women-headed households, often are not bound by traditional gender stereotypes that are more typical in traditional nuclear families. Men sometimes are present in these women-headed households as a de facto spouse, who may or may not play a significant parenting role, or occasionally as brothers, or male friends in a shared household. These women have a range of backgrounds. Lesbian mothers may involve the biological father of their child at some level. Young teenagers may have ambivalent, confused, or narrow ideas of gender stereotypes. Many single women are separated from husbands, are divorced, or have left a de facto. It is probably in this group that we find a clear liberation from traditional patterns of raising children. Indeed, many of these women have left men precisely in order to create more personal space in their own lives. A small group of single women are choosing to raise children quite alone. These women are often career women in their mid to late thirties, reasonably comfortable financially, who allow themselves to become pregnant with no intention of involving the biological father in daily child-rearing. These women generally reject traditional gender modes of child-rearing.

Individuality and distinctiveness

However families rear children, and whatever the presence or absence of adult men or women in children's lives, this issue of autonomous individuality, identity, difference, and diversity is crucial to most individuals in the late twentieth century. Autonomous individuality prides itself in the *distinctive*. At a superficial level, dress, hair, aesthetics, house design, cars, acquaintances, and lifestyle often conform to a particular subgroup, but all are statements of expressed individuality. Individuality permits eccentricity, the outrageous, the excessive, the refusal to conform, or a resistance to the status quo. Society clearly demarcates notions of 'normal' individuality, or at least of socially acceptable forms, and brands those not within its boundaries as deviant, delinquent, perverse, or irresponsible. This desire to express explicit individuality is often a central area of conflict in a household when for the first time a teenager plucks her eyebrows, dyes hair, wears extremist make-up, or rips jeans deliberately. These actions reveal an emerging identity expressing distinctive autonomy, often as a deliberate rejection of what has been offered in the home. Understanding the driving force behind these expressions may help families to be less reactionary to the frequently outrageous responses young people can make.

At a deeper level, learning how to understand our individuality, and feel comfortable with expressing our uniqueness, is an intricate process. Some individuals have been raised in families that accept a wide variety of expressivity—spontaneity, raucous outbursts, and crazy wittiness, as well as melancholy, quiet reflectiveness, and solitary musing. Other individuals have been raised in families with precise or narrow ideas of what forms of self-expression are permissible, and thus constrain most assertions, behaviour, or statements that fall outside the precise idea of limits. In these families, there is a considerable suppression of individuality so that individual family members rarely appreciate each others' differences.

The intolerance of many parents towards their children's developing personality often forces children to hide their friends away in their bedroom, or to escape out of the house where they can experiment more and be themselves. The realisation of the importance of this freedom often hits starkly when children have been out enjoying themselves, and walk inside their home, where narrow-minded circumscribed familial expectations are thrust hastily on them. It is not easy to accept that 'being yourself' might at times mean being moody, sulky, short-fused, humourless, austere, or distant, rather than being charming, gregarious, dynamic, pleasant, and very likeable. It is also not easy for parents to accept that their children may have personality traits they do not find appealing. Because of this reluctance of many parents to accept the different personalities of different children, many individuals leave home or travel, often going overseas in order to find out who they really are. Their aim is to start to express their individuality in situations where they hope they are not going to be judged or criticised. Many of us keep this uncertainty in adulthood, experiencing feelings of being cramped, restricted, and straitened by the presence of certain family members, and yet experiencing feelings of freedom and liberation when we are not with them. Other individuals spend a lifetime searching for who they are, always unsure of themselves, trying on personality masks, and changing the mask according to place, person, or whim.

To summarise, the autonomous self emerges in different ways for different individuals. Ideally, I am suggesting there needs to be a balance between an idea of the self as independent, as separate from others, and a recognition that this separateness is not in opposition to others, like with young Tom. Instead, one can be autonomous, and still prize our attachments to others. Indeed in a stronger sense, our connections with others are an important context in which autonomous beings relate, and through which our identity emerges. Both good and bad relationships in our early lives have a marked influence on our identity. The young boy or girl who is raped by a family member or a family friend has brutal scars on his/her identity that often take a lifetime to cope with, a harsh reality our families, legal judges, and societies are slow to accept.

Add *individuality* to this concept of autonomy and we have part of the unique excitement of being human, in that the expression of our self-determination takes many forms as people seek to assert themselves differently. I have suggested that this self-expression is straightforward for some, for others it is complex, uneasy, or awkward. Expressions of individuality reflect our autonomy. Within ethics, autonomy refers to the capacity for moral choice. An autonomous being not only has this capability for choice, but actually makes crucial moral decisions. In subsequent chapters we explore the implications of these choices for the quality of family life. But now let us try to understand more of how autonomous moral choice exhibits itself in the family.

Autonomous Individuality in Good Families

Why do good families need to foster a balanced notion of *autonomous individuality*, that sees the self as *both separate and connected*? How do well balanced autonomous individuals contribute to the well-being of good families? Do individuals with a strong independent self-expression really make a difference in the community?

Good families need to foster an autonomous individuality where separateness and connectedness are in fine balance. It is important that children grow up with a clear concept of their individual self-identity and of their attachment to others. We are who we are, as a result of our social narratives. Our lives are a story of intricate involvement with other people. These people are part of our history, and we figure in theirs. Relationships in our lives, those that have been significant and trivial, past and present, destructive and enriching, loving and hurtful, all influence our sense of who we are. We often struggle with the influence of these relationships and never fully understand who we really are. Some of us can live with this uncertainty and enjoy fresh discoveries; others of us wrestle continuously with self-doubt.

Beside the desirability of a balanced individuality, one which can cope adequately with the extremes of life—the joys and disappointments, those family members we get on well with and those we do not, the duties and the free choices—autonomy refers particularly to *moral choice*. Moral choice affects both the individual and others. Within family life there are a host of choices to be made. Let me stress that the sorts of choices I am talking about are not the everyday trivial choices like whether I shall have toast or cereal. The implications of choosing toast over cereal are not profound. They might cause minor skirmishes if I use the last piece of bread needed for school lunches, but nothing serious. The sorts of moral choices I am addressing are significant. They matter enormously. They will affect me, other family members, and other relationships in a profound way. The range of significant moral choices we confront is vast.

- Should I have an abortion when I know I cannot afford the costs associated with a sixth child?
- Should I tell my new girlfriend that I have slept with her best friend?
- Should I inform my mother that I saw my sister steal her pearls?
- Should I take part-time work so that I can collect the children after school even though the household budget tells me I need the full-time salary?
- Should I declare my bisexuality to my wife?
- Should I tell my aged father that the children are tired of his classical music which he plays all the time?
- Should I explain to my unemployed adult children that I cannot really afford to maintain them now I have been retrenched?
- Should I confront my brother-in-law about the suspicions I have about my sister's bruises, if she will not talk about it?

- Should I confess to my new husband that I really dislike my stepdaughter?
- Should I mention to my mother that I want to raise my children the way I choose to, not the way she brought me up?
- Should I tell my daughter her obsession with her bodily appearance is narcissistic?
- Should I explain to my son that his refusal to express his emotions scares me?
- Should I announce to my family that I am gay?
- Should I tell my mother I will not be having children, or let her keep hoping?
- Should I increase my child's pocket money so that it is in line with his peers?
- Should I confide in someone that my uncle is touching me in ways I am afraid of?
- Should I tell my cousin she is getting a reputation for being an easy catch?

The list could go on. You probably read the list and answered yes, no, possibly, probably, definitely not, I'm not sure. My point is that the family is a crucial arena for many moral decisions. These are not decisions made lightly. Much more than self-preference, ease, adherence to strict narrow moral rules, or just minimising fuss is necessary, for these are moral decisions that call on questions of the good. That is, what constitutes a 'good moral choice'? What practices enable us to flourish as moral identities? To remind you, right action is a product of our attention to the good. Our starting point is just to ask, 'what might make a good decision'? In the absence of universally accepted standards of goodness, it is the exercise of moral virtues that makes a person good. Sometimes we understand this only in retrospect, when we look back on our choice and say, 'that was a big mistake', or 'that choice made a lot of sense'. In wanting to make good choices, we might look to some of the virtues I am outlining in this book and ask questions like the following:

- Am I acting like an autonomous individual, capable of making up my mind in the light of those around me, able to explain my choice, and be accountable for the consequences?
- Am I trying to be inclusive to all family members, making sure I am sufficiently flexible, and negotiating with relevant persons?
- Am I being a faithful, loyal, and reliable family member?
- What does it mean to be faithful to my partner, beyond sexual fidelity?
- Am I being completely truthful, honest, and trustworthy in my family relations?
- Am I prepared to forgive?
- Am I being fair?
- Should I show mercy to a family member who does not necessarily deserve it?
- Am I adequately expressing my affection and my love?
- Am I creating a sphere of secure intimacy?
- Am I a good friend?
- Am I contributing to the interdependence of this family unit, or do I go my own individual way?
- Do we really depend on each other in a reciprocal fashion?
- How seriously am I taking my moral obligations to different family members?
- What degree of care can I reasonably expect from my family?

These are crucial moral questions we must grapple with. They are not easy questions. In fact, it is easier to shy away from them. But if we intend forging strong family ties, they are moral choices most of us will have to face at some stage of our family lives.

The Family as a Unit

Beside these important moral decisions that emerge in family life, primarily between two people—woman–foetus, mother–

son, brother–sister, or daughter-in-law to mother-in-law—there are other crucial decisions regarding the assertion of autonomous individuality that affects the family as a unit. There are three major ones I want to draw attention to—the division of household labour, family resources and finances, and chances for leisure and relaxation.

1 Division of labour

Who does what, when, is not just a simple management decision in a family, it is a decision influencing the good of family members. The allocation of household tasks is not just an assignment of physical duties, it is a statement of people's worth, of what others expect of them, and the responsibilities accruing. For example, not to give aged parents living with you some important tasks makes them think they have expended their usefulness. There are always some household tasks most elderly folk can manage. Moreover, appreciating their story telling, even if it continually harks back to their youth, is valuing their life experiences.

To assume that a woman should do all domestic tasks may make her feel like a housemaid. To tidy a child's bedroom when the child could do it does not teach that child important lessons about caring for personal property and being responsible for one's own actions. To insist that a man be the sole breadwinner and disciplinarian gives him an unwarranted and often abused position of authority and control. The division of labour in the house is a crucial moral choice. Where the household is more of an economic unit with small agricultural plots sustaining the family, all household members are responsible for some task to provide food, clothing, and shelter. When material needs are mass produced, the economy revolves around a monetary system. Waged labour earns money to buy what one uses in the family; often there is an emphasis on consumerism, and this undermines the potential for children to be seen as an integral part of household economic maintenance. It is important that the division of labour within a household is equitable, with all members participating according to capacities.

2 Family resources and finances

It is a myth to think that there is an equal distribution of family resources, even in households with a joint ownership title and where there are joint bank accounts. Evidence seems clear that the greatest contributor to household finance is usually a man, and he wields the most significant influence in deciding how much money is spent. What this tendency fails to acknowledge is the daily financial management women generally assume, and the enormous amount of unpaid labour most women contribute to the household.

In a materialistic society we only value what can be given a monetary value. Even in dual income families, the more a woman earns, the more she successfully uses this as a leverage to bargain for increased decision-making. For women who are not in the paid workforce, the housekeeping money is frequently their only access to finances. Where the government pays a Family Allowance, despite this being primarily intended to cater for the costs of children, it is for some women an important access to independent income. Separated and divorced women often report a satisfaction in having a new control over their income, however meagre it might be. What is important is not just household expenditure, but *joint consumption.*

3 Leisure and relaxation

Along with the division of labour and the distribution of resources, the third area of major choice affecting family units is the chances for leisure and relaxation. Who cooks when both partners work? Who does the washing up when all the children are out on various pursuits? Who gets the coffee when the family watches television? Who goes without when the costs of sporting and leisure activities, the movies and restaurants exceed household budgets? What about single parents, too tired or too isolated to pursue community baby-sitting options? Assuming that basic needs are met, decisions about ensuring that all family members have the opportunity to enjoy leisure are *moral*, not just managerial, for they affirm each person as having equal prospects of recreation and relaxation, and being equally worthy of due consideration.

Family choices

To summarise, choices in the family are important, as is the freedom to express who we are. Making choices that are consistent with our beliefs, temperament, and self-expression is an important part of our individuality. Good families need to foster strong autonomous individuality, and the confidence to express one's self-determination. The family unit is also an important arena for developing individual decision-making skills in major areas of life. The family provides ample opportunity to discuss the fourfold process:

- of considering options
- of making a choice
- of being accountable for the choice
- of being responsible for the consequences.

This process involves good and bad choices. A teenager who chooses to shop-lift usually knows this is wrong, and thus, on being caught by a shop detective, must explain the reasons for stealing and accept the consequences. A woman who decides to leave her violent spouse has to explain her rationale in detail to her children, to social security, often to schools, her relatives, and sometimes to his relatives when the children are fond of their paternal grandparents. Accepting responsibility for the consequences of this choice often means an enormous decrease in her standard of living. In this case, the good of her family's physical protection outweighs the difficulties of physical maintenance.

Good families are important units for fostering independence, individuality, and skills for decision-making. Yet nowadays the need to defend one's moral choice *in moral terms* is becoming a practice alien to many people; the mere self-assertion is seen to be sufficient. For example, a youth may plonk down by the television to eat dinner, saying he does not care about family meals. In this youth's eyes, there is no need to explain more, or be persuaded to join the rest of the family. A young husband may continue to sleep with his girlfriends, viewing this practice as his right as a man, without seeing this action as a choice that requires substantial explanation. Unreflective self-assertion almost always results in choices that disregard others' feelings.

Individuality and the Well-Being of Families

How do family members who are confident of their decision-making abilities contribute positively as moral agents to the well-being of good families? Assured of their own self-determination, they value the autonomy of others as self-respecting individuals, who are also capable of freely determining their own actions and behaviours. For these family members there is no need to dominate, or to control others, for they *respect the integrity of people's choices*. This is not always easy, particularly where strong-minded people clash. A toddler wants to wear pyjamas to playgroup. A child chooses to spend birthday money on a toy the parent does not approve of. A teenager chooses to smoke. A father accepts a promotion overseas. A sister flirts with her brother-in-law. In what sense should we respect these persons' choices?

Respect for individuality

A virtue at the heart of moral deliberation is *mutual respect*. This is a respect for all humans that the minimal ethical code outlined in Chapter 1 is based upon. Mutual respect involves a self-respect for one's individual agency as a person of moral character, and it acknowledges the autonomy of other moral beings. Mutual respect provides the groundwork for a life lived decently where we may need to agree to disagree. In the light of anticipated disagreement with others, it calls on more than toleration. It requires favourable attitudes towards those with whom we are likely to disagree. This attitude enables us to keep open about admitting to ourselves that our own views might be objectionable or even wrong. Being open also allows the possibility of our changing the positions of others we are confronting. Yet we need to try to recognise the moral force of others' positions. This means that we need to listen to the reasons people give for why they think their choice is right and good. We might not like their views, but we need to *listen*. How important this is in a family context!

My emphasis is on *moral reasoning*, not on self-interested bargaining. The issue is not 'do I like this view?' or 'does this view suit me?' but 'does it make good moral sense?' This emphasis makes possible deliberate choices of substantive moral values, thus contributing to individual virtue, to the family good, and to the social good. This position accepts that there will be fundamental moral disagreement, but that *open-mindedness* is important, and that where there is a striving towards agreeing how to handle disagreements, then we move closer to a view of the common good as something for which it is worth striving. Respect for individuals is therefore a social achievement, it affirms collective self-understanding. We explore in depth this respect and the lack of it in Chapter 10.

How then can we simultaneously respect the integrity of self-expression and of people's choices, and resolve dilemmas where the choices are, in our view, unacceptable, controversial, conflictual, immoral, or do not assist the growth of good families? Examples here could include the choice of our child's lazy partner, our sister's drug abuse, our brother's obsession with making money, or our husband's insistence on having sex when he feels like it. I suggest there are two principles that act as guidelines. They both rely heavily on the sort of practical wisdom I explained in the previous chapter, and a realisation that sensitive discernment is needed to assess when and how you intervene in someone's choice.

1 Learning through mistakes

First, we sometimes need to allow family members to *make mistakes*, and the older we become the more difficult this probably is. The proviso I make is that we can allow people to make mistakes so long as the *eventual learning* outweighs the potential harm of the mistake. Let us test this using practical examples.

If a toddler chooses to wear pyjamas to kindergarten, it really does not matter too much. It is only social convention being disturbed, not an ethical principle. Either the playmates will be totally accepting, revealing the nature of adult conformity to social mores, or they will embarrass the toddler, prompting the toddler to decide not to wear pyjamas out again. A teenager who chooses to smoke might be asked to smoke outside, might develop asthma or other respiratory disorders, or find a girl/boy friend who despises smoking. Parents might realise that if a teenager wants to experiment with smoking, they will, and that it is a lesser evil than harder drugs. Similarly, getting very drunk sometimes teaches teenagers to handle alcohol more carefully in the future. This does not mean we should encourage our teenagers to go on drinking sprees. It is acknowledging that we all make bad choices sometimes, and that sometimes we learn a lot through making these choices.

Kicking a ball on the road is dangerous, so this is not a lesson we ever encourage young children to learn. Having sex without contraception leads to the possible harm in an unwanted pregnancy, or where a condom is not used, getting AIDS or an STD, and hence is an unwarranted learning experience. But this first principle of *learning through experience* means that we need to make a wise judgement as to when family members might learn despite wrong choices, and when the choice might jeopardise any fruitful learning. Admittedly, it also assumes a willingness to learn that often does not exist. Children's seeming reluctance to learn can be very frustrating for parents who permit a degree of experimentation in the hope that useful lessons will be learnt.

2 Minimising hurt

The second guideline I suggest we use to help resolve dilemmas of conflictual family choices is to seek to *minimise hurt*. The father who wants the promotion overseas, despite the family being happy where they are, needs time to prepare the family for the possibility of a move, discuss options, negotiate over sensible times to leave, present the scenario of new openings and experiences that might emerge, making sure the eventual decision minimises hurt for everyone. The sister who deliberately flirts with her brother-in-law is in dangerous territory. She jeopardises her relationship with her sister, and is not taking seriously the fact that her actions will probably cause enormous hurt. In seeking to minimise hurt, we do not rush into choices, but consider how the choice might affect others who are close to us. This deliberation of options encourages an openness to considering others' views which is very important to the respect of others' moral autonomy.

Autonomous individuals in families and communities

Clearly, autonomous individuality contributes significantly to the well-being of good families. We need to allow for a wide range of forms of self-expression, and to respect the integrity of people's choices, and be aware that they will not always be the choices we would have chosen. As stated earlier, we need to permit family members, young adults particularly, to make their own mistakes only when the learning they achieve outweighs the possible harm of the mistake, an outcome not always known in advance. With decisions that might cause family friction, a resolution should aim at minimising the hurt of family members.

Divorce, a much needed legal avenue to free victims of intolerable and unsatisfactory partnerships, is one of the chief contributors to the sorts of tensions that create enormous hurt. It is children who often suffer the most pain in a divorce proceeding. A breakdown of family ties is likely when there is not a mutual respect for others. I go my way, and you go yours. The emphasis on autonomy alone ensures a freeing of relationships where choices are not made with consideration of their effects on others. This is why autonomous individuality, our expression of who we are as moral choosers, needs to be placed within broad social parameters.

Finally, do individuals with a strong sense of independent moral choice really make a difference in the community? The simple answer is, yes. People who from an early age have been encouraged to express their identity freely and to make important decisions in their private lives are more likely to be prepared to participate in the multi-layered form of decision-making which is necessary in the public sphere. A company's most valuable asset is its human resources. Empowering workers to make their own decisions, or to participate in co-operative decision-making, takes some pressure off central management. Good leaders encourage self-management as part of their quality management strategy. This includes all sorts of crucial choices in the economic world that invariably impact on family life, from senior policy and executive level to industrial relations issues concerning pay, work conditions, health and safety, to practical issues on the shop floor. It also involves deciding on personal issues like how many hours we work away from home, the distance needed to travel, and how much work we bring home.

Autonomous individuals stand up for what they believe, arguing their position against our youth glued to the television who act but refuse to take a reasoned position. Autonomous individuals will not be puppets, and will not accept what they disagree with. They will not submit passively to victimisation. As a result of their strong self-determination, they take more control of their lives, and accept personal responsibility for their choices. They ask important questions about what they want, need, value, and care about, and they act on their answers. Autonomous individuals scrutinise personal talents, abilities, values, and relationships, and frankly admit their strengths, weaknesses, and uncertainties.

This is the personal context in which to make choices that permit an active moral life to emerge. The sense of our own worth as a person means that our own considerations are given due weight in deliberation. Conscious of the need to choose well, self-respecting autonomous individuals act out their moral agency. Self-respect is a necessary part of moral autonomy, confirming our dignity. Similarly, affirming a mutual respect for others' autonomous individuality is a crucial part of moral life. What is involved in mutual respect is explained in more depth in Chapter 10.

4

Including All

In this chapter we look at how to include all family members. We look at what inclusiveness, flexibility, and negotiation mean in a family context, how these values contribute to the well-being of good families, and what differences these values make to community life. Inclusiveness, flexibility, and negotiation are intimately connected. I would go a step further and say that they are so connected that you cannot have one without the other. Certainly, you can include people in an activity and then be vindictive, alienating them and refusing to talk with them. But this book is directed towards developing positive relations. Therefore, if you try to be inclusive, you will have to be prepared to be flexible, and this involves negotiation with others. A willingness to negotiate shows an attempt to be inclusive, and a preparedness for flexible approaches. Most people who enjoy being flexible like to negotiate with others in order to include relevant persons.

Inclusiveness

Before explaining inclusiveness it is necessary to discuss its opposite. While communitarian societies value groups within the community, and deliberately try to include individuals in various groups, one of the key structuring principles in western individualist societies is exclusion. In these societies, there is a privileging of certain valued positions, and an exclusion of anyone who does not meet the requirements of these valued positions. These exclusive positions vary from culture to culture, but typically revolve around the association between masculinity, public citizenship, and material wealth. There are three areas pertinent to our topic in which exclusion is a key structuring principle—namely patriarchy, social structure, and family relations.

1 Patriarchy

Patriarchy assumes the authority, power, and control of women by men. In most societies men appear to be the centre of cultural value, having a power over women that has been culturally legitimated. The reasons for this are complex. One major reason is that men traditionally are associated with culture, the mind, the political, knowledge, logic, instrumentality, and dominance. Under patriarchal conditions women are *defined in opposition* to the traits valued as masculine, and thus come to be associated with characteristics like nature, the body, the personal, opinion, intuition, expressivity, and submission.

How does this cultural valuation and devaluation influence men and women in everyday life? Given that the traits associated with masculinity are the culturally esteemed traits, all men, regardless of their actual position in society, possess some power simply because it is assumed they possess some of these traits. Generally, it is men who hold positions of power as breadwinning household heads, in politics, business, industry, finance, education, the police force, and the military. These men have their status, power, and masculinity simultaneously reinforced. Indeed, some men actually associate their masculinity with their dominance, particularly over women. In the west, patriarchy adopts typical male frameworks like emotional distancing, calculative objectivity, and public procedural formality as ways of operating that are normative, or relate to the way society should be.

In contrast, women are excluded from many valued social positions because they are perceived to have developed skills inappropriate to the public world as men have defined it. Social recognition is granted in the public sphere with its material rewards and visibility. Consequently, traits perceived to be feminine are undervalued in society because they are seen to be more appropriate to the private sphere. Women in general are undervalued. Patriarchal structures present an exclusivity of a valued masculine position.

While much of this patriarchal exclusion remains, feminists have done many positive things to alleviate the burden of this exclusion. They question the rigidity of male and female roles, and the strict association of traditional masculinity with the public realm, and femininity with the private realm. Feminists also ask why traits traditionally assumed to be feminine have been excluded from public arenas and normally undervalued. Through centuries of child-rearing, women have a wealth of experience of nurturing and caring for others, and being sensitive and acting co-operatively in non-hierarchical, inclusive ways. These are important modes of operating, and should be included in the public arena, as well as in the domestic realms.

2 Social structure

The second area of major exclusion that affects families occurs within social structure. Social structure refers to patterns of relationships within a social system, such as what each society values. In a materialistic world, status, power, knowledge, and material rewards are prized. The exclusive nature of the prize creates divisions between the 'haves' and the 'have-nots'. The 'haves' possess social status gained through educational qualifications, specific knowledge and information expertise, access to scarce rewards, comfortable salaries and work conditions, opportunities for leisure, and a lifestyle of options for their children.

The 'have-nots' are excluded from the opportunities and realities of the 'haves'. Those who experience inequality, injustice, unemployment, and poverty, suffer extreme marginalisation, sitting on the periphery of society, not fully involved in active citizenship. Social structures perpetuate social exclusions with enormous practical implications for families in terms of economic security or insecurity. Yet many of the so-called 'have-nots' realise the ultimate poverty of a materialistic pursuit, and enjoy an active citizenship of a different, often simpler kind. Also, the children of many 'have-nots' often are determined to change their situation and defy social exclusion in subsequent generations.

3 Family relations

Thirdly, families themselves frequently exclude, sometimes as a deliberate practice, more often unwittingly. There are many examples. Parents or adults in the household often exclude children. It is rare for adults to exclude children entirely, but all adults need free time and breathe a sigh of relief when children go to bed. But there may be significant exclusions in areas whereby children's inclusion would be beneficial, such as in areas of decision-making that may have a profound effect on everyone—like moving house, changing schools, or having a grandparent come to live. Dinner parties are usually enjoyable, especially when they are free from hassles with children, but children are excluded frequently from the joys of special meals, becoming used to conversation-free meals, sprawled in front of the television. Children who deviate from family norms often are excluded, not only from family activities, but from parents' wills. This is particularly evident in upper-middle-class families where a child opts out of following in 'daddy's footsteps' as a barrister, doctor, diplomat, or businessman. Some children initiate their own exclusion, refusing to participate in joint family activities, unaware of the hurt this may cause.

Then there are male and female divisions in certain families, where mother and daughters, father and sons side with each other, each excluding the other from close interaction. Some of these dilemmas have had to be resolved by the homosexual community. Bisexual and gay men occasionally care for children from a previous relationship. Lesbian women who opt for artificial insemination have to undergo new reflective modes when they give birth to a son. In addition to gender divisions, in some families there are divisions of older siblings versus younger ones, the older ones deriving certain amounts of power in being able to exclude young siblings. I used to get frustrated by my older siblings taunting me by withholding information as to where they were going. In some families the oldest and the youngest take prime place in a parent's eye, irrespective of the sex of the child. In many cultures the eldest son as heir is honoured, and the rest are excluded.

Changes in family relations create new excuses for exclusion. When a new partnership is formed, the family of origin of both partners often are excluded in the early years of the relationship. This usually changes as children are born, and one's parent becomes a grandparent. Change becomes complicated if this partnership dissolves and a new one begins, again the situation is made more complex when both new partners introduce new children. In blended families there can be conflicts of exclusion between the two sets of children, between children from a previous relationship and children born to the new family, or between children and their non-custodial parent. Step-relations have always been construed as difficult, thanks to inaccurate persistent myths of the classic mean stepmother.

New forms of exclusion emerge with new types of families. The young upwardly mobile professionals (yuppies) with their clear aspiration to material wealth, career success, fashion style, and hedonistic lifestyles may be very intolerant of those people who cannot achieve such financially comfortable lives. They often cope by excluding the rest of the world from their everyday parameters. The double income no kids (dinks) group exacerbate these exclusionary tendencies. These people often argue against any policies that support universal family allowances. They ask why they should assist those who choose to have children. Families are often very exclusionary.

Exclusion makes exceptions, it omits, it evicts, it rejects. *Inclusion* is its opposite. It actively considers the interests of everyone in the group; it does not want to leave anyone out; it tries to insert family members into the activities. It refuses to have one exclusive orientation of, say, the father's position or the matriarchal grandmother's view. Rather, it listens to everyone's voice, and tries to make a space for *each family member to have a valued position*. An important part of being inclusive is being flexible.

Flexibility

Flexibility in a family, like a piece of elastic, bends and stretches; there is *give and take*. It does not say, 'this is my view, I won't budge'. Rather, it says, 'this is what I think, but tell me your side of the story'. Now this does not mean that we compromise on moral principles or household agreements. What it does mean is that we call on our fount of practical wisdom, and decide where it is appropriate to adjust our first command to something more reasonable. In straightforward issues this is simple. 'Do the dishes now' might be adjusted to 'please do the dishes when you've finished the puzzle'. The older children are, and the more complex the issues, the more difficult this adjustment becomes. Certainly we need to adapt our requirements of household help and family expectations to the different maturity levels and physical health of family members. But a request that 'you must tell me whose party you're going to before you leave home' might go unanswered, promises of phone calls unfulfilled, agreements to be a moderate drinker broken, and parental concern mounts. Parents' willingness to be flexible may not be appreciated; they give and the children take. A similar situation may occur between partners, or between siblings.

Flexibility also means that we are *open* to admitting we are wrong or should change. This does not come naturally for most of us. When we are flexible, we are able to be persuaded that something other than what we have originally decided is possible. Most of all it means that we are amenable to change, we are likely to listen to others' stories. A fear that all teenage parties are drunken orgies may, after persuasion, be modified to a belief that it depends on who is at the party, and whether an adult is present. Even those of us who are authority figures in the family are still accountable for our actions and can be judged on the basis of them. This means that we need to be very responsive to others, being willing to yield when necessary.

We are not going to be able to be so flexible that we can include everyone all the time, but nor would we want to. Parents need time out for themselves; children like playing without a parent's continual watchful eyes. Older people enjoy young people's company, but sometimes need the quietness of their own age group. Teenagers are not slow to tell adults when they want to be included and when they do not. 'Why can't I come to the restaurant?' is quickly followed by a 'but I don't want to come out with your friends, they're boring, so why should I?' There are clear life-cycle differences when children will feel delighted or even privileged to accompany adults; at other times they will be embarrassed. Demands of school, age, and health also limit flexibility.

Flexibility has its *limits*, or its *boundaries*. Even elastic will snap when pulled too far. Keeping sight of the boundaries beyond which we should tread warily, or never venture is important. Yet it is often difficult to know where the boundaries lie. Sometimes we jump the boundaries, dodge them, or bump nastily into them. However, some limits need to be set. Children should be reminded of the limits of times to be home by, people to mix with and avoid, and illegal, addictive, or harmful substances to refuse. If we are forever flexible, adapting constantly to everyone's demands, something snaps —family rules, tempers, the limits of moral reasonableness. Without understanding the need for boundaries, there is no limitation to behaviour or actions; everything seems permissible, so there are no moral constraints. Educating people to think about limits calls for a sensitive adaptation to different contexts, and a willingness to negotiate the boundaries. Often this willingness is absent, and so give and take, negotiation and meaningful flexibility, break down.

Negotiation

In wanting to include as many family members as possible, and in wanting to be as flexible as required, intricate negotiation and consultation strategies are necessary. This is time-consuming and often exhausting, but the importance of *discussion* in family life cannot be overstated. In *listening to other people's views*, we often become more flexible ourselves. The willingness to listen keeps us open to possibilities. We learn new things ourselves. Obviously this responsiveness is not always reciprocated. Just as the desire to be inclusive is often frustrated by social exclusions, so too the desire to be flexible might be restricted by having to work with dogmatic family members. The willingness to negotiate might be blocked by stubborn people who will not consult with others, or arrogant people who push their own views, or young adults who refuse to take advice, or parents who have always maintained their supremacy.

Negotiation presupposes potential disagreements. A willingness to negotiate involves an *exposure of one's own position*, perhaps initially in a tentative manner. Diplomats around the conference table cautiously declare their positions then, as confidence in each other grows, more and more of the specific details surface. The central aim of negotiation is to come to some *mutually acceptable agreement.* Frequently this involves compromise of one's original position, we rarely get exactly what we want in life, but the aim is to keep negotiating until some consensus is reached. The teenager who wants to stay out until 1.00 a.m. hears her mother say midnight, and they agree on 12.30. This is a gross simplification of a typical scene that may be enormously conflict-ridden, and where no mutually acceptable agreement is reached. The teenager sneaks in through a window drunk at 3 a.m.

The inability of many family members to resolve potential conflicts and tensions of family life contributes significantly to violence, discord, screaming and yelling, youth prematurely leaving home, partner separation, and divorce. Negotiation implies a readiness to talk, to give and take, and to come to some sort of agreement that is satisfactory to both parties. When any part of this difficult process breaks down, negotiation fades away.

Inclusive, Flexible Negotiation in Good Families

In discussing the benefits of inclusiveness, flexibility, and negotiation for the creation of good families I am assuming a merging of these virtues. A single mother who wants to include her children in many decisions and activities of significance, generally is prepared to be flexible and to negotiate. A lesbian who wants to include her partner in co-parenting needs many hours of negotiation and flexible adaptability not only to her partner's position, but to the situation of the sperm donor, in terms of his future involvement with the child. A household trying to include a newly widowed aged parent needs to be very responsive to his changed needs and to negotiate new frameworks for all to operate with. The step-siblings in a new blended family need to work hard at the practical mechanics of flexibility and negotiation to ensure that they all are included adequately in the new family unit. An elderly lady whose niece's mother has just died might know that her niece would like her to act as a substitute grandmother to her children. A divorced couple who want to maintain civil links because of their children must negotiate and be flexible. A formal court order establishing procedures for custody does not take into account contingencies that crop up, like the school expulsion, the sudden bike accident, or the conviction for arson. A child may just need to see or speak to the non-custodial parent, so open lines of consultation are important.

Those who conscientiously try to combine inclusiveness, flexibility, and negotiation contribute to the well-being of good families in many different ways. They make each person feel important, and affirm their moral worth as an individual to the family unit as a whole. Watch a small child's eyes light up when it is her turn to decide what dad should cook for dinner. Being prepared to negotiate with individuals shows that you are prepared to listen, and to take their viewpoint seriously. This certainly makes parenting more difficult. It is easier to be dogmatic. Negotiation is important in relations of equality and in relations of inequality, the latter being more typical in family structures. Between spouses, between a parent and a child, between a child and a senile parent, or between the eldest brother and the youngest sister, there are varying degrees of power and powerlessness, control and dependency. These differences alter the capacity to negotiate well.

A willingness to negotiate breaks down some of the inhibitory dimensions of power. It also increases a tolerance to others. When you are prepared to listen to others' points of view, you might not like the view, you might disagree with it drastically, but at least you can try to understand it from another's point of view. A youth's argument that the parent should be pleased the youth is 'only' smoking dope, not taking hard drugs, may seem ludicrous on initial hearing, but may make some sense after due consideration. The youth may be making a plea that s/he is not all bad, and could be a lot worse. Yet, as I have already mentioned, there are limits to how flexible we should become. Determining the precise nature of these limits is extremely difficult. Certainly there is the benefit of retrospective knowledge, of accumulated experience, and of wisdom with age. We all make mistakes. When to enforce, when to advocate, and when to leave limits open remain a perplexity for practical wisdom.

Another asset of the attempt to be inclusive, flexible, and willing to negotiate is the broadening of experience that results. Often children are excluded from all but childish activities, deprived of the opportunity to make a significant contribution to decision-making and negotiation, and deprived of participation in major celebrations. In cultures that are not communally inclined, where activity is geared to the public individual, the family is not always welcome in restaurants, bars, cafes, or coffee shops. Children are often treated as nuisances. Where children have the opportunity to be exposed to areas of life not typically available to their sex, age, and stage within the family, horizons are broadened, tolerance for diversity is increased, and family life enriched. Children who have witnessed christenings, weddings, funerals, and other major family celebrations gain perspectives on life's horizons, seeing birth, life, and death as part of a continuum.

Communication

Aiming towards inclusiveness, flexibility, and negotiation in families teaches necessary skills of *communication*. Where there is no attempt to negotiate, there are misunderstandings, closed communication, distortions, or stubborn dogmatism. As Jürgen Habermas, writer on communicative ethics, states, good communication aims towards speech that is comprehensible, true, appropriate, and genuine. Under these conditions, the goal is to communicate sincerely. A true conversation is an *open dialogue*. It presupposes some agreement between the participants, but there is always unpredictability, the novelty of individual expressions, ideas, and reactions. When each family member is given equal right to ask questions, to give interpretations, and to make recommendations, what is happening is very important. We are affirming each family member as a person worthy of being recognised. There is thus a mutual recognition of each member as an important person. The orientation is towards mutual understanding.

When these open values are encouraged in the home it does make a difference in the community. Good habits transfer themselves from the private to the public sphere. Employers who are good practitioners in inclusive flexible negotiation are responsive to their employees' demands, listening to their requests and their needs, and are sensitive to those on the fringes. This may include junior members of staff, contract staff, part-time workers, and immigrant and refugee workers. The workforce must be willing to adapt to changing personal and social concerns to be flexible to family and individual variations. Citizens with highly developed skills of *communicative ethics* will be able to translate these skills into the requirements of participatory democracy. Democratic procedures are time-consuming. It is much easier to give orders, or to allot tasks. Listening to what others want or need is a much more arduous project, but necessarily so, where there is the attempt to include, to be flexible and to negotiate. The outcomes of such negotiations are usually better, since individuals are likely to be more enthusiastically involved in projects which they feel a part of. These are skills that should be learnt in the family.

5

Sticking Together

Good families should stick together and develop virtues of faithfulness, loyalty, and reliability. Mobile societies inadvertently make the practice of these virtues very difficult. To be faithful, loyal, and reliable involves some strong sense of commitment to something, whether this be to a person, a group, or an organisation. That is, we are faithful to a friend or to a spouse, we are reliable in a family context or to a work company, we are loyal to a cause or to a sports club. What all these examples have in common is something that *binds people together* in a mutual pursuit of goals, or a shared orientation. Without this joining together there is minimal commitment to each other.

Many of the factors that once bound people together, and demanded a faithful, reliable loyalty from people have dissipated. There are fewer family businesses that maintain their family ethos and personnel over many generations. The day when the village blacksmith was the blacksmith for all the villagers is gone. Most of our shopping is done in large, anonymous supermarkets, where the 'good afternoon, how are you?' and the 'have a good day' of the check-out assistant does not have the same genuine ring as the personal contact possible in the local corner shop, often operated as a family business, and where service reflects family loyalties. Another element of mobility comes with employment. Many of us change employment many times in our lives, moving from one work situation to another. In frequently changing our employer, we move our allegiances, divulging the secrets of the past firm and taking newly discovered techniques from our present firm to the next. Often our attitude to work is instrumental. We work to get money, or as experience for promotion and, in this context, worker loyalty is tenuous.

With sports supporters we see evidence of some of the most fanatical loyalties possible. The scarves, hats, and painted faces all exhibit devotion to a club. In the past, supporters of one team rarely changed their support to another team. But again, while the basis for this support may be religious or cultural, it is largely locational. You support the team in the area you grew up in. Mobile societies have changed the basis to this support. As youngsters many of us shift suburbs, states, or countries as our parents' employment alters. As young adults many of us move to go to college, university, or in search of freedom, or employment ourselves. As partners we often move about finding suitable, affordable accommodation for our growing families, then move again as new partnerships are formed, and various families are blended. We live in societies that accept the inevitability of rapid mobility. This extends our horizons and introduces us to the 'global village', but it is a major contributor to the minimisation of the sort of commitment that comes from long traditions of stability that are likely to result in faithful, loyal, reliability.

A general shallowness in social commitments filters into families. This is exacerbated by widespread individualism which encourages people to pursue doggedly their individual interests, and results in people having a loose attachment to social groups, including the family as a social unit. Individualism encourages people to pick and choose according to preference, and this includes the option of choosing not to be faithful, loyal, and reliable family members, or to choose to be faithful when it suits. The cry goes out, 'it's my right'. A night on the town is probably more fun than visiting a sick aunt. An older teenager who goes out every weekend and refuses to baby-sit for her parents who rarely go out, does not consider the consequences of her behaviour.

Excessive individualism changes the basis of our priorities —the individual self takes precedence over the good of social units, and this works against the general well-being of families. This form of individualism removes much of the impetus for actively pursuing virtues of faithfulness, loyalty, and reliability, for individualists have a prime motive for satisfying self-interest. For families to stick together and show their commitment to each other, more than self-interest is needed.

The impetus for maintaining the well-being of families comes from ensuring that all family members are cared for.

Faithfulness

For those of us strongly committed to developing good families, what does it mean to be faithful? We talk of a 'faithful dog', or that 'she's very faithful to him despite his flings', or that 'he's very faithful to his religion'. So what do a faithful dog, a faithful partner, and a faithful believer have in common? What they share is a devotion, a determination to remain true, consistent, and dependable. The dog who chews his master's slipper is screamed at, whacked with a rolled newspaper, sent outside in the cold, is fed, taken for a walk, faithfully comes back at a whistle, and at night lies curled up by the crackling fire, looking up at his owner for attention, a picture of devotion. Religious believers listen to mockers questioning their faith, and remain loyal to their religious profession. The woman hears the rumours of her partner's flings, sees the lipstick on his shirt collar, smells foreign perfume on his body, and despite her sadness, remains true to him.

Sexual fidelity

The latter example is particularly pertinent, because generally faithfulness in a family setting is presumed to mean sexual fidelity if not exclusively, then certainly in the main. The permissive 1960s perpetuated the idea that sex is merely another form of play, that faithfulness is repressive, if not irrelevant, and that freedom is everything. The 1960s licence to pursue anything that might turn you on has come and gone. What has remained is an expansionist space for women's sexual expression. Reliable and readily accessible contraception has increased women's sexual freedom enormously. Sex no longer leads necessarily to pregnancy. Reproductive control is within the wider context of women's autonomous self-determination, and more women are initiating sexual relations, sometimes in addition to those relations with their prime partner. These activities are in defiance of the double standard that said women should remain faithful to their men to ensure the paternity of their children, while men have unbounded physical passion that needs more outlets than one woman alone can provide. Some people see it to be acceptable for men to have a steady partner and numerous casual affairs.

Is women's increased sexual freedom a good thing? Yes and no. Control over women's reproductive capacity is crucial, as is reproductive choice. Being free to decide whether to have a child or not, or to decide whether the continuation of a pregnancy is responsible or irresponsible are vital decisions self-determining women must make. Being free to initiate sex in an active manner is also a good thing rather than women being merely passive recipients. The opportunity to escape from repressive or destructive sexual relationships, particularly in marriage, is also a good thing, as is the exposure of the hypocrisy of the double standard. While it is contentious, some people might say that men and women alike should be free to have sex with whoever they please when they please. Is this further evidence of the seduction of individualism filtering its way into personal relationships? This seduction states that self-interested satisfaction alone dictates life choices, and this is all that matters. If the double standard is wrong, then it is equally wrong for men and women in that it jeopardises faithful relations.

Anyone who has been in a committed partnership where one partner breaks the fidelity knows the tremendous personal hurt this causes. There are the typical lies, the excuses for late dinners, the unexplained phone calls, the silence of the phone when the partner claims to be working back late, and the bizarre uncharacteristic behaviours. And then there is the discovery—the credit card bill for dinner, flowers, a hotel room, a letter in the top drawer under the underwear, the rumours, the chance sighting, and then the exposed facts. Suspicion, anger, bitterness, and deep hurt accumulate, as does a crushing sense of rejection, that one is no longer desired, no longer the prime lover. In earlier chapters we established that our concept of self is confirmed through interaction with others in such a way that affirms us for who we are. Rejection of the self is more than personally humiliating;

it stunts personal growth. It is the ultimate exclusion, a spurning of one's self.

In a context where AIDS is not just a political debate but a reality in people's minds as they contemplate sex with others, there seems to be a public confusion as to whether sexual promiscuity really has decreased, or whether it has decreased among certain sectors of the community. Those who are in a stable relationship are now more cautious about extra sexual relations for fear not only of catching AIDS, but of being caught out. This fear is particularly pertinent to bisexual men, and heterosexual couples who also indulge in casual sex. If this change is occurring, and a new commitment to monogamous relations is happening, then we need to ask whether this is a movement to sincere commitment, or just a frightened sociological response to the AIDS crisis.

Does a faithful commitment necessitate sexual monogamy anyway? Can we be committed to several people in differing ways and in differing degrees without jeopardising the qualitative level of commitment? If we think we can, how do we cope with jealousy, possessiveness, and the idea that sexual relations are a unique sharing, that we cannot give of ourselves totally to several people? It is true that some people draw on other sexual or emotional partners to delay, or to avoid facing various obstacles in their prime relationship. If we were to argue that multiple sexual relations are entirely permissible, it is difficult if not impossible for this to work without real problems. In the homosexual community, where individuals do not have children, some claim they can have deeply committed multiple relationships and that it works as long as each knows about the other. Nevertheless, the complications are not hard to imagine.

For example, in the heterosexual community one man may live with his spouse and children during week days and with his mistress at the weekend. Can the wife and mistress ever accept the fact that this man is controlling the situation, that the wife is not at liberty to approach her husband on Saturday, nor the mistress on Thursday? Another man, afraid of commitment, may have different women for different nights, privileging the woman who is given the extended weekend. Some career-oriented couples choose to minimise their involvement with each other by having quite separate lives, leisure pursuits, and even households, but are faithful to each other as exclusive sexual partners. This is a modern form of commitment. The union between *commitment* and *faithfulness* appear to go hand in hand.

One reason why such a union is not fully appreciated is that there remains the idea in many people's mind that the institution of marriage, legal and de facto, is an infringement of independence and freedom because it requires considering someone other than oneself, and because it gives faithfulness priority. Faithfulness is a legitimate expectation informing the way partners treat each other, that is, they do not deceive each other. Rather than restricting us, faithfulness can be liberating. It can actually broaden our freedom, for we can trust our partners, allowing us to have close friendships with either sex, without these relationships being seen as threatening to our prime relationship.

This opportunity for friendships between men and women is particularly relevant now that more women are in paid labour. Women often have been jealous of men's daily contact with work colleagues and secretaries who are generally attractively dressed women. Many affairs begin in the workplace. Giving each other the freedom to pursue close friendships allows both partners space to develop new and interesting contacts, and the security of knowing the value of the primary relationship. It validates our trust in each other. So faithfulness in families does not just concern sexual fidelity. Sexual fidelity might stand as a basis for a broader notion of faithfulness, but *being faithful* includes characteristics of devotion, consistency, and dependability, and it extends to other more general virtues, like loyalty.

Loyalty

When we hear the word 'loyalty' we often think of a strong allegiance to a nation: 'he's a loyal patriot, a true son of his country'. Or we read in the papers that the 'loyal fans' of a particular soccer club destroyed the opposition's club house. These forms of loyalty exhibit a fanatical allegiance to something with a long history or mythology, therefore they are extreme forms of attachment. Loyalty to something involves specific responses. In the family, appropriate responses might be faithfulness, constancy, dependability, and devotion.

One of the most conspicuous examples of loyalty is a family's devotion to a member who is ill, physically or mentally handicapped, or going senile. The response of an individualist who is only concerned with personal desires is to thrust loyalty aside. Loyalty frustrates the pursuit of self-aspiration. The easiest, most convenient, response of an individualist to the suffering of others is to institutionalise a cancerous daughter, a spastic brother, a schizophrenic aunt, an arthritic mother, or a father with advanced Alzheimer's disease. Here we are caught in a bind. On the one hand we are very grateful for the provision of professional care and expertise, a necessary respite from continuous domestic, caring service. On the other hand, we recognise that along with the institutionalisation of care is a depersonalisation, diminished chances of touch and warmth, less human contact, loss of familiarity, and colder and alien environments. In many cultures the idea of institutionalised care is an anathema—you look after your own.

It is a commitment to loyalty that largely explains the devoted care, usually from a mother or the oldest daughter and sometimes a daughter-in-law, to those requiring intensive care. How else do we explain a woman's sacrifice of her own career and interests to care for her adult child who is incontinent, must wear nappies, has to be spoon-fed, continually dribbles, must be turned in the bed every few hours, and can only grunt and respond to music? We read the stories in magazines, our hearts are filled with warmth at the extent to which human devotion can go, and we are thankful for our healthy family members who do not require such concentrated stretches of our time and energy. For those women who are devoted to the task of care there is enormous sacrifice. They often give up the pursuit of a career they enjoyed, or would have liked to pursue; their leisure time is non-existent, their isolation from the world outside their caring sphere quite extreme. For these loyal carers mental and physical exhaustion is very draining.

On another level the forcefulness of loyalty may restrict people's options. Take for instance cultural groups who demand their sons and daughters marry someone from the same racial, ethnic, cultural, and religious backgrounds as themselves. The defence of this demand is understandable. These parents desire a continuity of language, tradition, cultural customs, and an affirmation from their communities that they are maintaining loyal links with their culture. But the passions of romantic love are culture blind. A total close-minded tribalism refuses to see this, and often cannot see other options. A Chinese woman falls in love with an Afro-American man and both their parents ostracise them. A Protestant and Catholic couple talk in Belfast of what possibilities lie ahead for them. A Sikh becomes interested in a Muslim. A blond, blue-eyed German who is travelling, meets a woman from Bangladesh who hears of the rise in Fascism, and is too afraid to live with him. Multicultural societies attempt to integrate various groups. We enjoy the exposure to new food, new forms of music, art, literature, theatre, and dress. When it comes to uniting families, cultural loyalty often prevails over cultural diversity.

Loyalty has other positive features and avenues of expression. It makes us defend family members from outside criticism. Your little brother might annoy you enormously, but no one is going to call him a 'freckle-nosed twerp' to your face and get away with it. Loyalty to families might mean that we do things we might not do for anyone else, like shifting household furniture on a boiling hot day, attending the funeral of a bitter old aunt that everyone despised, or taking in your brother's rebellious daughter to give him a break from daily hassles. Loyalty is based on a *deep attachment* to something, and it requires proof of the attachment. Morality is active. We prove our loyalty by *being loyal*.

Reliability

Faithful, loyal family members are also reliable. Reliability has many practical implications for families. There are countless household tasks that need to be done. It is difficult for one person alone to do them, a situation in which the aged and the single parent frequently find themselves. Reliable family members are dependable: you ask them to do something, and they do it. They promise their children they will take them ice-skating and they fulfil their promise. Their word is to be trusted; it is certain to be true. These are honest people. You know they are reliable because of your experiences with them. They are unfailing in whatever they have committed themselves to do, to be, to promise. How do you know this? Because they are 'tried and true', they have a record of reliability. Many of us may have good intentions; we aim to do something, but when the crunch comes, we procrastinate, or make excuses, or find something more pleasurable to do. No one is reliable in the abstract. Reliability is an *active notion*, you demonstrate reliability by *being reliable*. It is a developed habit, it contributes to us being good persons.

Faithfulness, Loyalty, and Reliability in Good Families

As with many of the virtues being discussed in this book, these three virtues of faithfulness, loyalty, and reliability are interrelated. It is true that we can all think of exceptions to this interrelationship. Someone may be committed to sexual fidelity and loyalty who is notoriously unreliable. Someone else may intend to be loyal but is embarrassed about family connections, so finds it hard to show loyalty. Generally, the person who is faithful has a *character disposition* to be loyal and to be reliable. The loyal family member often exhibits loyalty by being reliable and faithful. The reliable individual aims to be both faithful and loyal. Break down one of these virtues and the others often crash down.

The woman who has harboured bitterness to her de facto partner's stream of sexual pursuits prior to their relationship sleeps with his business colleague when her partner is away. She is not remaining faithful to her partner who has been faithful to her over the last ten years. In doing so, she jeopardises her reliability. Her partner no longer trusts her when he goes on his frequent business trips. Loyalty to the relationship is threatened. For it to be maintained, there needs to be a commitment to the partnership, or to the family unit, for these virtues are difficult to maintain in an individualistic milieu where one is thinking only of oneself. These virtues give evidence of an *attachment* to family members, by being dependable in a family context. This attachment has definite ramifications for the broader community in three main avenues.

1 Family care

First, families that are committed to these virtues *care for their own*. Care takes many forms, from the typical daily care requirements we all need, to the special requests to assist in times of hardship, retrenchment, unusual situations, and sickness, to extremely demanding situations of disability, very old age, and very ill people. This care is a high priority, a sign of commitment and devotion to those who are family, even if it is at a high personal cost. This provision takes considerable pressure off the state in having to provide care.

Yet there are numerous individuals and families for whom the availability of public care is essential on an occasional, respite, or permanent level. This includes the care of the severely disabled, mentally disturbed, or ill, as well as individuals who through no fault of their own have no other family members willing to provide the care needed, and those who are homeless, destitute, alcoholic, or mad. A good society ensures there are *minimal thresholds* below which no individual should ever wander. This minimal requirement is particularly pertinent for individuals who are not part of loyal family networks. It should make societies feel ashamed knowing that some of its citizens live in bus shelters, tunnels, or cardboard boxes, foraging in garbage bins for food.

Modern welfare does attempt to satisfy a wide range of basic needs. As the writer Michael Ignatieff reminds us, we need more public debate on what people 'need in order to realise the full extent of their potential'. These needs include aspects of a humane life that public care finds difficult to provide, like 'fraternity, love, belonging, dignity, and respect'. Good family care should provide the framework in which these important human needs can develop.

2 Community care

Secondly, and in a related way, fostering faithful, loyal, reliable family members contributes to the likelihood that these individuals will extend a sense of attachment beyond the family and make a positive contribution to community involvement. As state welfare provisions shrink further, voluntary community work is becoming increasingly necessary to maintain the requirements of *community care* in a broad sense. This ranges from sports coaching in schools, to transporting the aged to shopping centres, providing meals for those unable to cook for themselves, and giving respite care to those long-term carers of difficult, uncontrollable children, or the severely handicapped. Those who offer their assistance in the community have usually developed these faculties in their own families. Their contribution is seen as an extension of their family involvement. A father coaches a soccer team his son plays in. As non-custodial father, this gives him a little more welcome contact with his boy. A mother who has had difficult children of her own and has learnt good coping mechanisms, remembers the value of outside help and volunteers to foster unruly adolescents.

3 Dependable workers

Thirdly, the development of character traits of faithfulness, loyalty and reliability in the domestic sphere are crucial traits for the public sphere, particularly in terms of paid employment. From the highest politician, senior executive, and professional, to the street cleaners, the garbage collectors, and the cleaners of public bathrooms, the economy thrives on *dependable* workers. Such workers are consistently reliable, they are punctual, take off only the permitted tea and lunch breaks, and they work with a dedicated constancy. This is not a picture we can all relate to. We buy goods that break quickly. We contract labourers who do a quick, expensive, and shoddy job, and as paid workers ourselves, many of the more noble dimensions to work are not uppermost in our hearts. Many of us work to pay the bills, keep the mortgage afloat, and to feed and clothe our children. Good loyalty requires good working conditions. When this exists, there is likely to be a loyalty to the work context and, this might mean a commitment to a family business, an institution or organisation of social repute, an educational institution with a tradition of excellence in learning, or a manufacturing plant with a determination to produce quality goods. In the absence of these motives, workers' motivation to be faithful, loyal, reliable persons regularly fades away.

To conclude, the development of faithfulness, loyalty, and reliability in families creates the foundation for a strong sense of *commitment* to other persons, groups, and organisations. It is based largely on a sense of *attachment* and our *practical actions* validate these attachments. We are more likely to have strong attachments where there is a long sense of tradition building up these bonds. Socially mobile societies work against the continuity of social relationships that are necessary for these traditions to accumulate. In being aware of the rapid changes societies are undergoing, we need to be diligent in developing the virtues that may counter some of the erratic forms of social relationships.

6

Being Truthful

Let me tell you a childhood story. We lived opposite a reserve with a park. I had been playing at the park, found some money and brought it home in jubilation. For some reason nobody believed me. They all accused me of taking it from my mother's purse. Her purse with her housekeeping money was always in the top drawer in the kitchen. She trusted us. I was upset by the accusation, and by the fact that no one believed my story, that I had found it on the sand under the jungle gym where older children likely to have loose coins hung upside down.

I can laugh over this little story now, but perhaps it contributes to the strong importance I place on the need to be truthful, the integrity of honesty, and possibly the most crucial virtue in any relationship, that of *trust*. To highlight this point, take as an example our children's activities—it is the lies, the deceit, the broken trust that often is more obnoxious, and more immoral than the activities themselves. Children repeatedly learn the stormy way that it is not worth breaking hard-fought-for trust. When trust has been violated it is very difficult to re-establish, for we are always a little nervous with people who have disappointed us. Yet curiously, how many people do we really trust? How many people do we trust wholeheartedly? How many family members do we trust with our confidences, or know will care for our deepest desires or pains? Our spouse? Our mother, stepmother, foster mother, adopted mother, grandmother, or mother-in-law? Our father? Our brother, sister, colleague, or friend? Whom do we genuinely trust, and how honest are they with us as they explore the truth of the hurt, the disappointment, and the grief of life, as well as the hope, the joy, and the celebrations?

As we explore these virtues of truthfulness, honesty, and trust in more depth, remember that the practice of virtues make us good persons. It hastens the movement toward the social good of fostering a family's well-being. Given the enormous complexity and contradictions bound up with human relationships, we rely on practical wisdom, good habits, and good judgements. We learn to be truthful, honest, and trustworthy through *being truthful, honest, and trustworthy*. We learn to create good families by being good families. What I am stressing is not the ease in achieving these goals, but the need to *strive actively towards the goals*.

Truthfulness

'How many biscuits did you take?' asks the child's mother's boyfriend. 'Two' screams the child, stuffing the third in his mouth as he scuttles outside. 'You're the first person I've slept with since my marriage broke up', croons a woman to the man she lies in bed with, fearful, knowing he works in the same department as another man she slept with last month. The men meet in a coffee break at work, both suspicious of each other when the woman's name crops up from the mouth of another workmate. 'Don't know her well', they both claim. 'All the investments will be ploughed back into economic growth for the nation', reads the transcript as a businessman stands to trial convicted of massive fraud. Truth, or the lack of it, weaves its way from the triviality of biscuits to the personal complexities of sexual relationships, to the public exposure of corrupt business ethics.

'Are you really telling the truth?' we ask a child. 'Is that true?' we ask incredulously as we hear something we can hardly believe. What are we actually asking? What does it mean to value the truth? What is truth? It has a lot to do with the virtues we have already discussed like being faithful, reliable, and loyal. Truth has particular qualities attached to it, and particular practices are needed to ensure that truth prevails.

Qualities of truth

First, qualities associated with truth include the motivation to be sincere, to be genuine, and to maintain fidelity to standards. An antique dealer wanting to know whether a chair is a true antique, a faithful example of a Victorian craft with genuine hand-stitched tapestry, has a gauge of quality of Victorian furniture in mind before declaring it to be a true antique. What then are the standards of truthfulness we maintain in personal relationships that allow us to assess whether someone is telling us the truth or not? The standards relate mainly to honesty, which I expand on shortly, but it involves not being given to lying, or to creating false or misleading information. Truth is the straightforward opposite to falsity. We know a person is telling the truth when that person is not lying, is sincere, is genuine, and is faithful to principles of honesty. It is not always easy to judge truth. Let us look at six variations where truth does not prevail.

1 Direct lies

It is very unsettling when people who are close to us deliberately lie. We want to be able to trust these people. A niece lies about her husband's mistress to protect the children who have guessed anyway. Our sister lies and says she has not borrowed our brother's CD player, yet no one else was at home. A son lies about his drug habit until he is found stoned. A grandson lies about stealing his grandmother's purse, but he suddenly buys people presents. An aunt promises to take her young niece to the zoo, says that she is sick, and is seen playing tennis by her oldest nephew. These are examples of direct denials of the truth.

2 Distortion of facts

It is difficult to judge the truth when facts are distorted. The principal of the school your adolescent son attends has telephoned informing you that your son and three of his friends were absent from school from lesson four on. When your son returns home looking tousled and bothered, you query him on his day's activities. He first claims he was at school all day, then when he hears the principal has rung, he tells you he was not well, so he left school, felt sick, lay down in a park, fell asleep and has just come home. You ring the parents of one of his friends whom you know well, and the story there is that the boys had been given permission to use a community library, became enthusiastic and stayed longer than they should have. Neither parent knows what to believe. Truth is distorted.

3 Misleading information

A single father with two young sons has chosen to work part-time to increase the time he has to care for his boys. He is in a highly-paid profession working as a specialist consultant in a medical centre. Nevertheless, it is a substantial drop in income for him and he decides to sell his house with all its memories of his estranged ex-wife, and build a smaller house with a bigger back yard. The builder is an old school mate, so while they agree on the contract for the structure of the house, many of the financial extras of fencing and landscaping that were not written into the contract but that he thought they had verbally agreed on are thrust on him. A 'gentleman's agreement' is broken. They argue. Misleading information has led to a major misunderstanding and conflict.

4 Unintentional untruths

Two Japanese backpackers are lost in an English-speaking country. A helpful policeman on the corner of the street misinterprets their question of 'where are the nearest toilets?' and sends them off in the direction of the Council sewerage plant. A child screams out 'quick mum, I've got two minutes to catch the next train, what time shall I return?' The mother hurriedly scrummages into her handbag, checks the timetable, yells out a time and the child races out. The door slams and the mother realises she has given the weekend time, not the weekday time. In both instances, there have been unintentional untruths told, yet the motive to assist was pure.

5 Withholding the truth

A woman is finding it increasingly difficult to manage the household budget. She shops carefully and saves what little she can. She is entirely reliant on income given to her by her spouse. He gives the appearance of being generous, but always makes her feel guilty when she buys anything for herself. Yet he enjoys seeing his children dressed smartly, and playing with expensive toys. He has a vast wardrobe. This man has a history of gambling which broke his first marriage. His present wife is disturbed to find a host of betting tickets in the pocket of a pair of trousers she is cleaning. She is horrified when she realises he has been betting a higher amount each week than he gives her for food and household maintenance. On trying to broach the issue, he tells her it is none of her business what he does with his hard earned money, and slaps her across the face. Truth is withheld.

6 *Truth glossed over*

To continue the above story, our gambling businessman feels some remorse over having slapped his wife whom he loves. He does not like to see her crying and miserable. He appreciates the way she keeps the emotional wheels of the family churning in a harmonious manner. When he tries to comfort her she just wants to know the truth. The truth is that this businessman cannot give her more housekeeping money because he is in substantial debt, mainly because of his gambling. He is betting high stakes in the hope of a big win that will clear his debt, but he is getting further into debt. He does not want to tell her about the financial mess he is in, and so tries to reassure her by saying, 'we'll be all right dear'. He wants to believe it is his own problem that he will solve, but it has many ramifications for the family. His wife knows this, but is too afraid of his temper to argue. Truth is glossed over.

We have probably all been victims of, and perpetrators of:

- direct lies
- distortion of facts
- misleading information
- unintentional untruths
- withholding the truth
- truth glossed over.

Nevertheless, the qualities of *truth* require us to maintain standards of *honesty*, to be *sincere*, and to be *genuine*.

Practices of truth

Secondly, as well as *qualities of truth*, there are *practices of truth*. People who speak the truth are often frank, forthright, and straightforward. A young doctor who has to tell her patient that the operation she has just had means she will never be able to bear children cannot dodge the truth. She cannot tell direct lies, distort the facts, give misleading information, tell unintentional untruths, withhold the truth, or gloss over the truth. As a doctor, she can only be frank and straightforward and tell the truth in a way that is as sensitive as possible. Similarly, there is no kinder way for a policeman to knock on the door and inform parents that their child has been killed in a car accident than to be kind, frank, and straight with the facts.

To be forthright need not entail aggression. It means we are clear about what we want to say, and we say it in a very direct, honest, and straightforward manner. This direct truthfulness covers information given to children on their bodies, discipline requirements, household expectations, career potentials, job prospects, advice on school subjects, friendships, contraception, romance, and financial budgeting. Clearly, being forthright and straightforward could result in a crude bluntness. 'You're nowhere near good enough to make the top team' might be true, but it lacks the sensitive flexibility that practical wisdom requires. 'You've really improved in your fitness, but you'll need to practise your kicking and ball control if you want to be selected for the top team' is less harsh. Truth matters.

Honesty

Being honest is a crucial part of *being true*. An honest person is not prone to lying, cheating, or stealing. Obviously there are exceptions. A woman in a war-torn country who steals an extra bowl of rice to give to her child does so for a worthy motive—the preservation of life of her kin. We do not doubt that under civilised living conditions, she would in honesty pay for her rice, or exchange something for it. A terrorist arrives at your door asking for your high-profile spouse who is a judge and you lie, saying she is still at the Family Law courts. Again, we justify these lies on moral terms, saying that while lying is generally wrong, not sustaining a life, or taking a life is more wrong, and sometimes we need to make ethical choices that rely on spontaneous practical wisdom. These are exceptional examples. For most of us, the prospect of starving in a war-torn country or having to face a terrorist is not likely to happen.

On an everyday basis, it is important to know that the people we live with are not stealing, cheating, or lying. We despise the anonymous thief, the top bureaucrat who has misled the public and pocketed public monies, but we can distance ourselves from their muddy affairs, which only affect us indirectly. There is something very unpleasant and very unsettling about being surrounded by family members who are lying or stealing. We know it is happening, the youngest child has his piggy bank stolen, a family's weekly luxury item of a packet of chocolate biscuits disappears, a hole appears in the lounge suite and a burnt cigarette butt appears on the carpet, and nobody owns up to it. Your daughter informs you that she is staying at a friend's house, but this friend's mother telephones to check on her daughter's whereabouts. Dishonest people are not trustworthy.

Honesty on the other hand brings out virtues of frankness, openness, sincerity, fairness, straightforwardness, honour, and integrity. These are good qualities because they mean a person is trustworthy. To the question, why be *truthful*? or why be *honest*? the answer is, because it means *you can be trusted.* It is comforting to know that you can have complete confidence in the words and behaviour of those with whom you associate closely.

Trust

The practice of trust means there is a *reliance* on someone, a faith in the worth, truth, or reliability of that person. 'Oh you can trust him' means you can rely on this man, he does what he says he will do, he is quite reliable. Trustworthiness defines qualities of character. A trustworthy person is ethical, dependable, principled, responsible, steadfast, honest, truthful, and to be trusted. In a family context, there are numerous instances of the need for trust, from the small expectations of requiring a child to return the change after buying milk, to being able to rely on family members to help out when other family members are sick, tired, or highly stressed, to more intimate forms of trust like depending on someone not to betray your confidence after you have poured your heart out and confessed your anxieties.

Trust is important at all stages of the life cycle. Children need to be able to trust parents, whether they live with both parents, with one, or away from their parents. When this trust does not occur, childhood fear and distrust, bred in lies, deceit, and broken promises, can lead to an adult life of perennial suspicion and an emotional distancing, with those adults who are affected, never daring to get too close to someone for fear of having their trust betrayed. But parents are not always to blame. Children also break trust. Parents need to be able to trust their children. While children are growing up, there are many lessons to learn. A parent with an untrustworthy child keeps hoping the child will learn to be honest, truthful, and reliable. Explanations, and another chance to prove that trust is warranted, sometimes are sufficient, but at other times the cycle of broken trust continues. There are mistakes of youth that are easier to excuse than when they occur in a young adult, or in an adult who should know better. A parent who loves a child, but cannot trust him/her is sorely grieved. Trust between lovers also is crucial; it grounds the relationship in bonds that expand beyond the physical. As I explain in Chapter 9, trust is the hallmark of a genuine friendship, the stamp of authenticity.

Yet not all trust relationships are good. Your daughter decides to bypass school for the day, and depends on your son to cover for her. Big businesses, crime syndicates, Mafia-type groups depend on high degrees of reliance on each other to carry out their dubious dealings. What sort of trust is worthy of admiration? Annette Baier, moral philosopher, develops a clear argument to answer this question. It is based on the idea that the human soul's activity is *caring*. She argues that no one is able to look after everything—ourselves, our relatives, the children many of us have, our pets, our possessions, and our gardens. Sometimes we have to trust the care of those things or persons dear to us, to others. Beside these tangible things, from time to time it is too much to hold on to our innermost thoughts, and we need to trust the care of our fears, anxieties, and desires to a confidant—our fear of men that comes from sexual abuse by a grandfather, an uncle, a father, or our belief that all women cannot be trusted because our alcoholic mother lied to us daily, or our debilitating shyness with new people, or the insecurities we have for any number of reasons. In sharing ourselves in this way, we are saying that we cannot hold all things in ourselves, that we need to have others share in their release.

Trustworthy parents hold a number of goods in their care—children's physical protection, shelter, warmth, nutrition, clothing, health, education, psychological stability, spiritual nurture, and loving attachment to others. Children are entrusted to parents' care, and children rely on the competency and willingness of parents to look after, rather than harm them. With the birth of a first child particularly, the weight of this care is often felt almost as a burden, the terrifying uncertainty of caring for a totally dependent baby. Society does little to educate prospective parents. This example highlights a significant factor associated with trust, a certain *vulnerability*.

In trust, there is a handing over, a *reliance on another's goodwill* but, as Baier puts it, 'one is necessarily vulnerable to the limits of that goodwill'. She notes that we often come to appreciate trust retrospectively, once our vulnerability is brought home to us by our actual pain. In opening our hearts to confess our wounds to others, our weakness is exposed along with our vulnerability. We experience trust when another has listened, has cared, has empathised with us, keeps our confidences, and follows up with appropriate care. Trust has to be earned. We do not trust uncritically; we trust when we have due cause.

Baier adds another useful qualifier. Trust is morally decent if, in addition to what is entrusted, knowledge of each person's reasons for *confident reliance on the other* can also be entrusted. For example, you can imagine an old lonely woman confiding in her single middle-aged daughter some secret from childhood that ties the two together in a tangle of guilt, and which forces the daughter to stay at home to care for the mother. This is not a morally decent form of trust. If, on the other hand, a couple have joint custody over their children, based on the fact that in the early years of the children's lives both parents were prime carers, then some trust will need to remain. Despite the impaired relationship between the adults, each parent needs to transfer custody of the children they care deeply for to the other parent. Knowing they both truly care for the children cements the trust, so the parents can rely on the quality of care, even if their lifestyles are quite different—she may live the life of a suburban housewife, he a bohemian artist on a boat. This form of trust is morally decent. The reason for parents' trust in the other is that they both care for the children, and because they both exhibit responsible caring, the trust itself is above suspicion. These children can slip easily into regular domesticity with their mother, and non-conventional spontaneity with their father.

Truthfulness, Honesty, and Trust in Social Contexts

Truthfulness, honesty, and trust are critical virtues in late twentieth century culture, where lies, insincerity, fakes, dishonesty, cheating, stealing, falsifying, and unprincipled untrustworthiness often prevail. A youth laughs in gay abandonment at the ease of shop-lifting and the parental reproach that it is wrong. A business company launders innocent investors' money, continuing to declare minimal dividends. We have seen many instances where the lack of truthfulness, honesty, and trust in families contributes to severe hurt, disappointment, and feelings of being let down. The flip side is that families are also an important agent for encouraging individuals to be trustworthy. I want to outline four other areas where these virtues matter:

- social context
- professional context
- economic context
- political context.

By looking at the importance of virtues in these four contexts, we will affirm the three major arguments of this book, that:

- good families are important
- our private and public lives are intertwined
- good families encourage good citizenship.

1 Social context

Our social lives are important to most of us, providing a welcome break from life's mundanities and necessities, a chance to relax, enjoy ourselves, and enhance our quality of life. Friends make up a big part of our social lives. Often the more friends we have, the more diverse is our social life. Some of these friends will be loose attachments, part of a sports club, for example, where you might not know the club members well on a personal level, but where trust is a central feature of the association. You must be able to trust your team members to attend practice consistently, to be disciplined, to be reliable, to be supportive, and to play as well as they are capable of playing. Schools often moan about the lack of commitment in their sports clubs without seeing that children are rarely encouraged to view their involvement in sport in moral terms—as a form of mutual trust, that is, something they can rely on each other to do to their utmost capacity. Beyond these loose attachments are our closer friends, those who are very dear to us. Trust is a central feature determining the quality of these relationships.

There are three main levels of sharing that test truthfulness, honesty, and trust. First, there is the general level of information you give someone, like news of a pregnancy, a changed job, or intentions to buy a house. News moves mysteriously, and it is very frustrating to hear someone else recall news clearly gained from your friend, but somehow the truth is distorted. You are suddenly expecting triplets, not just a baby. You are suddenly manager rather than clerk. We need to know that our friends will give honest accounts of information, and that they can be trusted with our news.

On a second level, there are the confidences we share with friends, like the domestic violence we are enduring, the uncertainties of retrenchment, the loss of virginity, the grief of a miscarriage, the unwanted or the planned pregnancy, the illicit affair of a married woman, or the life-enhancing affair of a single dad. We share these things for different reasons, needing to tell someone, wanting to share the joy or have others ease the pain. Whatever the reason, it is crucial that our friends are honest with us, that they do not fake their responses, that they give a truthful account of their reactions, and that we can trust them with our confidences.

This sincere reaction is crucial at the third level, where we really unburden our souls and share our innermost self:

- that we are tired of hiding the fact that we have had a criminal conviction and done time in jail
- that we have never cried
- that we have never stopped grieving for our stillborn child
- that we cannot forgive our sister for hurting us as a child
- that we regret deeply our non-attendance at our father's funeral
- that we retain bitterness at our brother's callousness
- that, despite our high-profile job, we have always had a failure complex
- that our stepfather was so cruel that we grieve for the natural father we never knew
- that death terrifies us.

When we cry on our friend's shoulder and share these deep inner thoughts, we must trust their ability to handle us and the disclosure in a sensitive way. This may be asking a lot of our friends, particularly when the news is unexpected or disturbing. We often require from our friends total confidentiality; we trust them exclusively with these startling exposures of the self. Some of us avoid disclosing our inner thoughts because we do not know people whom we can trust exclusively. Those friends who have developed a positive sense of autonomous individuality as outlined in Chapter 3 are likely to be able to handle these sensitive exposures of the self.

2 Professional context

Beyond the familial and the social there are professional contexts where trust is paramount. We all put ourselves, the children we may have, or our relatives or partners in the hands of professionals—educators, medical staff, accountants, lawyers. When we send our children off to childcare, kindergarten, school, college, or university, we have a reasonable expectation that those in charge can be trusted to treat them fairly, not to be cruel, to develop their talents, and not to sexually abuse or harass them. Think of the enormous trust that occurs between doctor and patient, between doctor and nurse, between nurse and patient. While we have come to revere specialised knowledge, more of us are acquiring broad knowledge bases and we accept a culture of critique whereby we do not take professional knowledge for granted, but we accept that it is legitimate to question professional strategies. While we may query the doctor's procedures, diagnosis, prescriptions, or suggestions, ultimately we trust the integrity of those who have taken the Hippocratic Oath promising to aid healing. Perhaps surgery is one of the maximum forms of acceptance of professional trust, where we allow another to anaesthetise and to operate on our bodies.

Lawyers and journalists often work in the muddy undercurrents of life extracting information from people not known for their honesty, like criminals, and people who have transgressed legal, business, and moral codes. A lawyer defending someone who has clearly committed a crime travels a fine line between defence of the client who may be dishonest and legal codes of ethics. Journalists use various means to extract their information, again hovering on the borderline of legitimate ways of handling informers, dubious sources, and unreliable hunches, but rarely disclosing confidential informers. There are professional codes of honesty that lawyers and journalists are subject to.

3 Economic context

A third area where truthfulness, honesty, and trust are important is in the economy. A capitalist market economy operates on the basis of the profit motive, and of efficiency as the goal that frequently is unworried by the means by which it is attained. Given widespread abuse of unethical corrupt means, and the realisation that people do not trust a company that has an image blurred by such corruption, there is an increased recognition of the need to take business ethics seriously. That is, market relations and contractual exchange between mutually self-interested parties can benefit from truthful, honest relationships, rather than a calculative instrumentality that is not bound by moral codes. Business dealings are not always noted for their trustworthiness—the quick dollar, pound, yen, or deutschmark, the grubby notes under the counter, the box that fell off the back of a truck and is sold down a dark alley, the business lunches, wining and dining to gain some idea of what each has to offer: the big dealers—the exchange and commodity share markets, manipulating the economy at large, the greedy corporations, banks, media magnates, and property dealers ruthlessly fighting for material maximisation.

Trust softens the harshness of market relations, but it involves many players. The elderly couple wanting to invest their life savings in a financial shares portfolio must be able to trust their advisers legitimately. The retailer must trust suppliers to forward required goods. Property dealers trust the surveyor's reports that the land is not a marsh and foundations will be firm. This attempt to instil truthfulness, honesty, and trust into market relations involves more than ensuring economic efficiency. It ensures that market relations are attempting to be moral. Trust modifies the calculative instrumentality of economic dealings, and gives a human dimension to what is typically a formal market exchange. Where there is this moral dimension, economic relationships are more likely to involve a sense of responsibility, and of not wanting to disappoint the other party. Truthfulness, honesty, and trust are important moral dimensions to economic relationships.

4 Political context

Trust is crucial in politics. Government structures are experiencing a legitimacy crisis. The political apparatus is overloaded and the state is not always clear as to what it can reasonably include within its parameters. All sorts of interest groups direct their attention to the state in order to extract financial support, or lobby for changed legislation, or for public exposure of certain issues. We vote and trust our leaders to legitimate the state's operations. We expect our leaders to be morally responsible, to be trustworthy, honest, and truthful. Our political representatives are expected to be public examples of morality, which is why the media loves to sensationalise both the private scandal of the politician caught with a call-girl, and the public scandal, the politician diverting political party funds to finance official overseas trips with attractive secretaries. Political trust is lost when political parties fail to live up to their promises of eliminating child poverty, of increasing welfare benefits, of improving public housing, public health care, and state education. The need for politicians to be accountable to their constituency is an important way of maximising their adherence to goals of truth, honesty, and trustworthiness.

Why be truthful? Because it is part of self-integrity, and you will be considered as honest, and as dependable. Why be honest? Because we can trust honest people. These virtues are crucial in the public sphere where our actions are necessarily accountable to others as social citizens. Where *truthfulness, honesty,* and *trust* are encouraged in the domestic sphere, these virtues are more likely to flourish also in realms beyond the intimate sphere. This transference improves the quality of our friendships, the integrity of the professionals we deal with, the morality of the market place, and the accountability of our politicians.

7

Treating Others Well

Forgiveness, justice, and mercy are virtues concerned primarily with the treatment and the *well-being of others*, but there is a difference with these virtues compared to the other virtues we have discussed. The need for these virtues reflects the *frailty* of human existence, that no matter how noble our intentions, how much we try to be good, we fail, and we fail often. We all make mistakes in the way we treat those we live with. Sometimes these mistakes are trivial; they hurt someone for a short time and then they are easily forgotten. Beyond this carelessness in our everyday lives, these accidental insensitive breaches of conduct, there are the more insidious, intentional wrongdoings that make the person wronged feel a victim. When this happens, the hurt is significant; it is not something readily pushed aside like the newspaper headlines read over breakfast that affect a nation's problems, but from which we can distance our personal lives.

Mistakes made by those we live with, and mistakes we make that affect those we live with, have to be dealt with sensitively; they affect us in the here and now, and leave lasting impressions. To redress our shortcomings, we need to draw on virtues like forgiveness, justice, and mercy that enable us to respond morally in view of the weakness of the human condition. We need to accept that we:

- do wrong, and need to ask for forgiveness
- need to accept an apology offered to us, cease to blame the wrongdoer, and refrain from maintaining a sense of being wronged
- do not always treat people fairly
- sometimes discriminate against others without providing an adequate justification

- do not always treat people in ways that reflect a respect for human dignity
- are sometimes insensitive to the suffering of another, and do not act graciously.

The family is certainly an arena where there is ample scope for forgiveness, justice, and mercy to prevail. Let us examine some practical examples and what is involved in each of these virtues.

Forgiveness

Any talk of meaningful forgiveness must include the wrongdoer and the person wronged, a willingness to ask for forgiveness, and a willingness to forgive. Yet even this is complicated by some people who do not acknowledge that they have hurt others. I want to deal with the more trivial examples of the need for forgiveness first, then move on to those that have profound implications, for different activities require different levels of forgiveness. In most moral dilemmas where a mistake, an error, or an omission is made, there are degrees of moral blame.

Human mistakes

A husband may compensate for forgetting his wedding anniversary, because he feels terrible when he is reminded, by buying his wife red roses and French perfume. He can be readily forgiven. Someone who makes a remark at a dinner party that is meant to be humorous, but whose comment is quite cutting and definitely shoots its barb accurately, needs to apologise to the human target. Beside the personal hurt, it is a public humiliation. A child in his eagerness to help, clears the table, but piles up his load too high and the crockery crashes to the floor. Despite the price or sentiment attached to the broken plates and cups, we ought to forgive this child. His intentions were good; he wanted to help. We can certainly explain to him that he was carrying an excessive load, and we are disappointed with the breakages, but it is a mistake we might have made at his age.

Similarly, as adults, one partner might be taking on an unmanageable work load, and not coping with the stress this induces. The family can no longer overlook the fact that this adult is either frequently absent, or is present but irritable. To fail to recognise the sorts of mistakes we all make, and to withhold our forgiveness because in this instance we did not make the mistake ourselves, leaves us guilty of an unwarranted arrogance, and an intolerance of the frailty of human existence. So where we are talking of minor errors we all might make—forgetting someone's birthday, accidentally breaking something we borrowed, making a remark meant to be humorous but that had a harsh sting, not being thoughtful to those who are tired, ill, weak, dependent, or powerless, we all need to ask for forgiveness, and readily accept apologies from others.

Extreme wrongdoing

Then there are more extreme categories of wrongdoing, where people wronged would not dream of committing the act themselves, they feel like a victim, and harbour resentment against the person who has wronged them. The resentment is understandable, though not desirable. These serious examples might include:

- a woman whose spouse constantly ridicules her in public
- a sensitive young boy whose father rejects his affectionate gestures
- a single father whose daughter continually lies to him and steals from him
- a single mother whose brutal ex-husband stalks the area she works in, verbally harassing her, despite court restraints
- a man whose ambitious wife constantly reminds him that he never lives up to her expectations
- a well-behaved younger brother whose older stepbrother demands their father's time, energy, and attention, because the older brother's wild life leads him into continual trouble
- an ageing uncle who is lonely and needs attention, but who knows his young mistress has moved in just to persuade him to alter his will in her favour

- a family who faces financial hardship as a result of one family member's obsessive gambling habit
- a faithful spouse whose partner is having an affair
- a victim, male or female, of incest.

What all these examples share is a victim who has been wronged by another family member, and who feels some deep emotion towards the wrongdoer. This emotional response is not always understood by the victim, or consciously invoked. Nevertheless, the responses include anger, extreme disappointment, fear, shame, humiliation, hatred, confusion, bitterness, and resentment. Now it is important to remember that morality requires us sometimes to feel these deep emotions. Take anger, for example—when we watch on our television white people burning the homes of black people, we are legitimately angry at apartheid and wrongful assumptions of white supremacy. This is a morally legitimate anger that helps us to identify as wrong things like racism, injustice, exploitation and the existence of people living in squalor and shanties. In this instance, anger helps us to recognise evil and to avoid evil.

As an example of personal indignation, imagine our teenage son is bashed by a street gang and left unconscious and bleeding in the street. We are understandably angry at the senseless stupidity of the act. Our son was simply returning home from a film, doing no one any harm. If we passively visit our son in hospital, bypassing how his injuries were inflicted, we fail to identify the cause of the wrongdoing, that our son was an innocent victim of a gang's maliciousness. Realising his innocence, we might feel deep emotions toward the wrongdoers. If we doggedly pursue the street gang in order to get our revenge, and cut off an ear of every member of the gang, then our resentment and anger has overstepped its boundaries. If our son's victimisation has been widely publicised, and to our amazement, the gang sends cards and magazines, befriends our son, mends his bike and prompts the local council to start a community youth group, it is much easier to forgive their earlier actions. This example has an unusual happy ending. Relatives of people killed or seriously injured by joy-riders, drunken drivers, terrorists, rapists, thugs, or murderers may find forgiveness an impossible response.

There is a legitimate place in morality for anger and strong emotions. But hard feelings need to be kept within moral limits, and given human nature; this is more difficult than letting them fester. The electronic media abounds in the vivid exposure of racial conflict, 'ethnic cleansing', religious sectarianism, and all sorts of extreme examples of vicious anger: 'you burn me, so we burn you'. Even stronger, 'you are not my colour, culture or religion, but you are living within my national territories, so I will destroy you and those like you'. These expressions of anger exceed moral limits. Acknowledging the excess is a real test for victims of gross wrongdoers. It is why, understandably, black writers on slavery and subordination, or Jewish writers on the holocaust, often want to keep the anger alive, to contemplate forgiveness, but never to forget, so that we might identify extreme evil, in order to avoid it in the future.

Attitude of wrongdoers

Whether it is easy, difficult, or impossible to forgive often depends on the attitude of the person who has been the wrongdoer. It is considerably easier for us to forgive where there is *repentance*, or a *genuine change in attitude* of the wrongdoer. Repentance is not just a religious response. Repentant people will typically feel shame, embarrassment, remorse, guilt, humiliation, or regret for their actions and conclude that what they did was morally unjustified. Where there is repentance, wrongdoers experience some of these emotions. There is a change from someone who saw nothing wrong with mistreating you in the way they did, to someone who now disapproves of the behaviour they once considered to be permissible, or thoughtlessly engaged in.

Despite the obnoxiousness of the wrongdoing, it is relatively easier to forgive these people than it is to forgive those who say they are sorry for what they have done, but have not changed their actions significantly. Indeed, the child who comes up to her mother and says a quick 'I'm sorry', in order to get the weekend pocket money, but who clearly is not experiencing any of those emotions related to repentance, is probably not genuinely sorry at all. Either the child's moral character is not geared to being virtuous, or the child has not understood the nature of the act—that shop-lifting, although easy at times, is wrong, that taking drugs, although perhaps mind enhancing or a confidence booster, takes its toll physically, mentally and emotionally, or that continually breaking agreed curfew times is unfair to anxious parents.

In fact, the emotions of guilt, remorse, shame, humiliation, and regret are such unpleasant experiences that they act as a break to discourage us from engaging in actions that might produce these emotions. We are very uncomfortable when we are feeling guilty. We shift in our seats, avoid eye contact, and behave in ways that are out of character. But guilt comes with the acknowledgment that we have done wrong. Not all wrongdoers acknowledge their wrongdoing. Also, as we have noted previously, where there is not a widespread social consensus on morality, there is a diluted sense of what is right and what is wrong. Therefore, the same act may lead to deep guilt in one person, and merely slight embarrassment in an other person.

Moral boundaries

The boundaries between good and evil, permissible behaviour and restricted behaviour, have shifted, or are less clearly defined. Religion, law, social custom, and familial expectations once held them rigidly in place. The diminished rigidity is desirable, for, as we have noted, moral choice is complicated by different contexts, so some flexibility is needed. The boundaries between the morally worthwhile and the morally unjustifiable might need to move a little in one direction for one moral action, a little away for another. What determines this movement though is a sensitivity to moral ideas, and *an application of principle to context*, so that our practical judgement holds sway, rather than mere self-preference or an adherence to dogma.

This emphasis on *practical wisdom* is important, because when the boundaries are blurred, and the moral education of our children is not given the priority it deserves, many of our children lack basic knowledge of the sorts of virtues we are discussing in this book. I am suggesting that these virtues help to situate the *moral boundaries* that enable us to make *good moral choices*. Otherwise, we simply decide on the basis of religious rules, social conventions, or personal preference and individual choice. Using the logic of self-interest, co-operating with parents is sensible only if rewards accrue. On this logic, you present yourself as reliable only when it suits you. On this logic, shop-lifting is only wrong if you are caught, otherwise you get away with as much as you can.

When children grow up in societies with few consensual boundaries between morally acceptable and unacceptable behaviour, and few corresponding moral rewards and moral sanctions, they come to believe that they can act as they please. With many young people there is minimal awareness of what actions are dishonourable, and thus there is a significant absence of moral shame witnessed by acts of graffiti, vandalism, joy-riding, assault, robbery, arson, as well as a blatant disrespect for law enforcers, teachers, and parents.

The wrongdoer, the victim, and the context for forgiveness

Where there is remorse and an acknowledgement of wrongdoing, what does forgiveness mean? As mentioned earlier, the initiative should ideally come from the wrongdoer. But the person wronged must realise that a refusal to forgive leads to bitterness, a bitterness that maintains a vivid sense of the wrongs. I am sure we all know of people who have endured a lifetime of bitterness. The lonely old grumpy uncle who was jilted at the altar and never let another person get emotionally close to him has let one person's responses hinder the opportunity for warm relations with others. The woman who never had the chance for higher education, despite doing well at school, and who pushes her children, nagging about their homework and exams, and refuses them access to their grandparents, is still bitter, resenting her parents' suppression of her talents.

Forgiveness, from the point of view of the person wronged, is to realise that not to forgive means continuation of the anger, hatred, and resentment that accompanies the particular wrongdoings. Forgiveness requires that we abandon these feelings, after having faced them, because they do us harm. This is rarely a simple matter. Abandoning destructive feelings often takes a long time, but we do this because we want to relate to people with more appropriate responses. The type of behaviour we refer to influences forgiveness. For example, we readily forgive the child who is usually reliable, but who happens to be late for one particular meal. On the other hand, the partner who has had an affair for over a year, and who has caused us intense heartache, will need to prove their remorse. Trust takes a long time to rebuild. Gradually we accept an apology, we cease to blame the wrongdoer, and we are concerned with renewing right relations with the person involved.

Forgiveness thus is a moral virtue that does not let our resentment to those who have wronged us go beyond appropriate limits. In determining what the limits are, we have to draw on principles outlined in other chapters, like considering *context*, the degree of *harm* inflicted, and the *hurt* involved in not forgiving. Sometimes the limits are totally obscure, or so extreme, that we cannot forgive. The extent to which we can forgive totally, that is, when we can say, 'I wipe the slate clean, it is as though you never committed the act', depends on the nature of the act itself, time as a healer, where the person is genuinely sorry, and on the strength of the relationship. For certain acts, concerning certain people, we can never wipe this slate clean.

There is always a *context for forgiveness*. It is true that some people have a forgiving nature, but generally we forgive *specific persons* for *specific actions*, like our mother for being controlling. We forgive people who have repented and changed their ways. Our mother now enjoys watching us make our own decisions. In addition, we forgive the person who begs us for forgiveness, like our partner who has slept with our best friend, and implores our forgiveness. We forgive a person who has suffered enough, the alcoholic father we fled from years ago, but who has dried out, as well as our well-meaning sister who has always embarrassed us. Indeed, we forgive some people also just because of their history with us: a good friend, a lover, our child, our parents, someone with whom we have a long-standing relationship. This closeness sometimes helps us to excuse certain forms of behaviour more readily; at other times we apportion blame more severely. If people really know us very well, they should be more careful in their treatment of us. Sadly, some people have experienced more pain, hurt, and suffering in families than anywhere else. Yet sometimes we forgive those we know well even when they have not acknowledged their faults, or apologised for the hurt they have caused us. Forgiveness is a strong virtue.

It is standard religious teaching, adopted also by many non-religious people, to, 'hate the sin but not the sinner'. In forgiving, we do not condone the activity. We can still despise the activity: the abuse; the financial squandering of shared funds; the withholding of affection; the drunken violence; the destructive, addictive life-patterns; the foul mouth; the selfish inconsiderateness, but we abandon our hard and negative feelings towards the person. Sometimes the feelings remain, or return with unwelcome frequency. We occasionally read of remarkable stories where the partner or parents of someone who has been the victim of a terrorist attack, a murder, or a rape, grieves for their loved one, abhors the immoral act, but somehow forgives the attacker. This is different from granting a pardon. This is a legalistic notion where a person in an official position decides not to punish. It may apply to parents who feel they have every right to punish a child but, for any number of reasons, choose not to do so. It is *rarely easy to ask for forgiveness*. When we have been severely wronged it is *rarely easy to forgive*. Time alone often heals.

Justice

One of the reasons we often need to ask those we live with for forgiveness is because we have not treated them fairly; we have not acted justly. We have not always given our family members what they are due, and we have not granted them sufficient respect. As we saw in Chapter 3, self-respect involves a respect for one's own agency as a person of moral character, and a respect for the autonomy of other moral beings. Justice in a family context is not merely concerned with establishing formal principles of fairness, but it involves a commitment to heal broken relationships as a sign of treating people justly, as persons of integrity, and of moral worth. This is not a typical understanding of justice.

For political theorists, justice is a principle of social institutions, that because there are scarce resources in a society —resources of wealth, status, possessions, educational qualifications—and there are masses of self-interested individuals competing for these resources, there need to be principles of fair distribution. In a liberal democracy there is the assumption that there are equal rights to the opportunities available in a polity that enable one to claim the resources. Hence, a well-ordered society should have a regulated public conception of justice, with fair procedures for the distribution of benefits. So *justice* is basically about *distribution* (who gets what?) and it is concerned with *entitlement* (who deserves what?).

Debates about whether justice is a principle appropriate only to the public realm are contentious. Most political theorists agree that justice is a virtue of social institutions. The family is undoubtedly a social institution. The interplay between the public domain and what goes on in our domestic lives is intricate, with, for example, work commitments impinging on family life, and family crises disrupting activities in the work place. Economic costs, wages, and tax policies all influence family life. As a social institution, the family is an important site for justice issues, yet justice is not always an appropriate virtue in the family context.

Family as a site for justice

First, then, we look at how justice operates in the household in terms of distributive justice, and then we shall look at entitlement. Distributive justice takes into account factors like ability, achievement, merit, effort, sacrifices, actual contributions, need, and the requirements of the good of the community. It provides relevant reasons for treating people differently. In the community it might involve a special educational programme for inner-city children of the long-term unemployed. Not all children are receiving this programme, but they are not being disadvantaged by this. Rather, the target group have a special need justifying why they should receive this programme.

In the household we constantly distribute differently to different members of the family yet try to retain strong principles of justice. Generally we distribute shelter, warmth, and bedding equally, but we distribute food and clothing according to need. We may give pocket money according to the contribution children make, giving extra where extra effort is made, and rewarding special achievements accordingly. The most difficult dimension to distributive justice is an issue particularly pertinent to those of us who are parents, namely, how we work out criteria for treating family members differently. Children have an acute sense of injustice. There seems evidence for an intuitive sense of justice, a moral notion of what is fair and what is unfair. One of the early phrases children learn to say is 'that's not fair'.

On uttering this phrase, children often challenge adults' selection of the relevant criteria for treating people differently. It is often as trivial as a brother getting a bigger bowl of rice than his twin sister, the parents' assumption that the boy needs more nourishment, or a sister being allowed to climb the banana tree, while her younger brother has to have a bath. The boy does not understand that his parents think that he is not strong enough to climb. With my children, shoes are an issue. My two sons are very physically active and kick balls, skateboard or race about, and wear out three pairs of shoes a year. My daughter never wears a shoe out, so claims she should be allowed to buy very expensive shoes to compensate, otherwise 'it's not fair'. I point out the difference between need and desire and that she buys more clothes than they do. Parents are often caught in the 'do as I say' mode, without explaining why they are asking their children to do certain things, and why they require different things from different children.

Careful judgement is needed to decide when to treat family members differently and still remain fair. *Need* is a priority criterion for differential treatment. We give the sick, the hurt, and the traumatised family member specialised attention. Contribution is also an important factor to consider. The child who tries to be tidy, helpful, co-operative, and cheerful warrants special recognition or reward, in contrast to the child who leaves possessions lying about, never offers to help, is verbally abusive, and refuses to comply with household agreements. In the name of justice, we justify relevant reasons for differential distribution in the family.

Distributive justice also concerns major political questions of global injustice, famine, starvation, inadequate nutrition, health, and education, and in the industrial nations it concerns injustices regarding unemployment, housing prices, and the financial dominance of market consumerism. In the household it covers the opportunities each family member has to fulfil their potential as autonomous agents. The understanding of justice as a principle of fairness about who gets what breaks down when it is seen as something protecting the rewards of self-interested individuals, rather than as a principle regulating social life.

Where individualism predominates, an over-emphasis on individual rights refuses to see that fair procedures necessarily adapt according to context and persons, so that what is fair for your older supportive sister is not necessarily fair to your younger rebellious cousin. As mentioned above, the self-assertive claim by many older children, 'that's not fair', can often be interpreted as meaning 'I'm angry because I'm not getting my own way'. A self-interested interpretation views justice instrumentally, as a means to ensuring 'I'm going to get what I want, regardless of whether it's owing to me or not'.

In a context of rampant self-interest, the idea that *punishment* is a dimension of *just deserts* seems ludicrous. Many people do not appreciate that if a child steals, cheats, and lies to other family members, then that child can expect to be treated differently from the child that does not steal, cheat, or lie. Indeed, for those children, pupils, or employees that abide by moral codes, it is only fair that parents, teachers, or employers have just forms of punishment for the thief, cheat, and liar. In doing so, justice regulates social life. Without this regulation, the self-interested individual only sees the search for *who gets what*, refusing to see that the other dimension to justice is one of entitlement, *who deserves what*. And it is here that justice as a principle of fairness becomes very tricky.

We can understand it as an operative principle in the public sphere. Equal Opportunity policies, for example, endorse merit as proper to distributive justice. These policies assume that merit is insulated from the worst market forces and wilful discrimination, so that people deserving of positions get the positions. This does not always happen, but at least the endorsement of merit keeps principles of justice and of entitlement alive. But how can we decide between claims based on legitimate entitlement and need? Your landlord is entitled to the week's rent, but you need the money to feed the family. Herein lies a real dilemma. When concepts of justice are tied only to individual self-interest, entitlement is seen as an individual right, something that is yours regardless of merit or of need. The landlord thus justifies sending a debt collector. If either merit or rights alone dictate family mechanisms, there is a conflict of interests, and many aspects of family life like unselfishness, charity, pardon, and sympathetic attention go missing. In a similar way that I listed need as a priority criterion for distributive justice, so need may also influence decisions of entitlement.

Difficulties in applying justice in families

My second main point about justice in the family then is that justice as a social principle of regulation is not always appropriate in a family context. This is because justice as traditionally understood concerns impartial ways of judging the fair distribution of rights. Yet we are not impartial in the family, it is *particular people* we love, despise, or fear. We are implicated ourselves in the roles, we do not stand off as impartial observers. If your son comes crying to you saying his big sister gave him the smallest piece of fruit, and this is her second piece, you are not likely to stand back and apply only impartial principles of distributive justice. The particular requirements of the context will come to the fore, as will issues of fairness. The simple point is that the questions of justice do not arise in the abstract, but in real-life situations where an emotionally distanced impartiality seems out of order.

In the family it is not the entitlements of individual self-interested beings that is the prime concern, but *the good of the family unit.* Within this shared understanding, individual's claims make sense only in relation to the unit as a whole. Straightforward entitlement may take second place to something else. A single mother may be earning a wage, working hard, and feel as if she deserves to reward herself by buying a new dress, but her twins both get sick in one week and the dress money pays for medicines. Need takes priority over entitlement. A married woman carrying the triple load of paid work, unpaid domestic labour, and childcare may feel she is entitled to some help from her husband, but may endure her unfair load to keep the peace. Her legitimate entitlement is denied. A man may believe he has an unconditional right to use his partner sexually and that she is not being fair in refusing his sexual advances. She may give in to prevent the physical roughness that would follow if she refused him. This situation is not fair because the man's expectations and behaviour are unreasonable. Self-interest obstructs the good of the family unit.

Formal, abstract principles of justice alone are of little assistance in making good judgements about informal, concrete, particular situations in the home. In order to overcome the injustices that occur in families, we need to know details about, for example, the struggling single mother, her sick twins, the hard-working married woman, the insensitive husband, the physically aggressive man who defines his masculinity in terms of sexual dominance, and the woman who submits to him. Knowing the *particular details* about the people who are suffering injustices, enables us to make *good judgements about fair behaviour.* Power relations often constrain these judgements from becoming effective. We will explore this in more detail in Chapter 10.

It is a paradox of sorts that, while it is essential that principles of justice are taught in the family, it is not always appropriate that principles of justice alone reign supreme. The political theorist, John Rawls, claims that we need to establish principles of justice precisely because we cannot know individuals well enough for love to serve alone. Presumably with close friends and family members we aim to know each other well enough for something other than formal justice to come into play, something more akin to mutual goals. While the family may be unsuited to the exercise of formal claims of justice, it plays an important role in providing a framework where a sense of justice can develop, and where just habits can be learned.

Children must be taught to share, to divide treats and possessions fairly. Teenagers must be shown that part of being respectful to others is treating people fairly, and honestly, and that equity sometimes requires differential treatment. For adults, justice extends to ensuring the provision of fair opportunities for all household members to pursue a meaningful life that is consistent with mutual respect. The rigidity of the gender division of labour invites injustices. The paradox is that while it is important that a spirit of justice prevails in families, and that children are taught basic elements of fairness, often something other than justice is more conducive to creating good families.

In personal relations that are governed by affection and warmth, claims to my individual rights and to fair decision procedures that benefit me are often made secondary to a spirit of generosity, not obliterating competing interests, but making the relationships between others more important than individual entitlement at someone's expense. Without the foundation of justice, exploitation and personal tyranny may prevail. *Loving relations* should be *just relations*, but just relations in a family frequently pivot around more than justice, calling into our focus acts of mercy.

Mercy

Mercy is a special form of compassion. We observe suffering, we feel a distress for the suffering of others, and we assist people who have no real claim to our assistance, in the attempt to relieve their suffering. There is no formal talk of entitlement, of merit, or of deserts. Nor is there any obligation to forgive. Mercy is gracious; it is an unmerited gift. A story frequently told to illustrate the act of mercy is Shakespeare's *The Merchant of Venice*. Antonio signs a contract, promising Shylock he will repay a loan or Shylock may take a pound of flesh from his body. Antonio is unable to pay his debt, so his friends beg Shylock to accept late payment rather than a pound of flesh, that is, to act mercifully. Antonio's friends do not argue that Shylock should forgive Antonio, or that it would be unjust for Shylock to take his flesh, but they maintain that he ought to temper justice with mercy. In the end Antonio escapes from the contract on a technicality.

Herein lies the classic dilemma between *being just* and *being caring*, holding on to formal, abstract, impartial principles of fairness, and yet dealing with practical situations which often require informal, concrete, partial practices of care. Carol Gilligan, a feminist psychologist and educationalist, has written extensively on the relationship between justice and care. She argues that care, construed within a justice framework, is the mercy that tempers justice. Let me illustrate this. Your son has just smashed your car that was not fully insured. He has apologised profusely to you, and you have forgiven him. Nevertheless, you are upset, because as a long-term unemployed single father, you cannot afford to have it repaired. You know your son is saving to buy his own car, but these savings could help pay for the repairs. Your son is upset also; he knows he had one drink more than he should have, and he knows he has more savings than his father. The father, although distressed himself, feels the suffering of his son, and although he could make the son pay for his mistakes, (indeed it would seem fair to ask for a financial contribution), does his own mechanical repairs, making do with the dented car body, so that his son can keep saving for his own car. The virtue of *mercy tempers justice.*

People who never act out of mercy are cold, quite insensitive to the suffering or needs of others. People who are merciless are extremely harsh. In contrast, merciful people act from compassion for others, and treat them less harshly than one would expect to be treated given the circumstances. We do not haphazardly act from mercy; it is a chosen response to particular persons in specific situations. Because of the special voluntary nature of merciful acts, and because it is a differential form of treatment, the merciful person is open to accusations of injustice. This might sound strange, so let me explain.

Imagine a household with an uncontrollable son who refuses to accept any parental authority on curfew times, acceptable leisure pursuits, attendance at school, and who refuses to participate in household duties. In this household there is a daughter who is co-operative, helpful, and sensitive to the parents' difficulties in coping with her brother. The parents in this household are continually showing mercy to their son, assisting him in situations where, because of his persistent misbehaviour and blatant lack of respect, he really has no rightful claim to their aid. They do this because they love him and because they hope that if mercy is shown often enough, he will eventually modify his rebelliousness, and realise the strength of their forgiveness. The daughter, while understanding of this situation, resents her brother. In her view he is continually excused for inexcusable behaviour. It does not seem fair to her that mercy is shown with such frequency.

The reaction of this daughter/sister is understandable. Mercy and justice often conflict, as do other combinations of virtues. Although honest, we lie to the crazy axe bearer. Although reliable, we will be late for an appointment if we stop to help a friend in distress. These are easy conflicts. In terms of the conflict between mercy and justice, the hardest and most contentious thing to work out is which has priority, and when it should be a priority. To continue with our example, from the girl's point of view, in making mercy a priority, justice is diluted. We generally demand of our judges that they prefer justice over mercy in dealing with criminal activity. But this highlights a crucial difference between justice and mercy.

Justice is primarily a virtue within the public realm, and while we need an underlying just milieu in personal contexts, these contexts also require appeals to the particular, the sympathetic, the compassionate, the charitable, the kind, the gracious, and the merciful. It is precisely the practice of these particularised virtues that makes family life unique—a special arena different from the world of absolute, inflexible principles of fair treatment of others. Yet undoubtedly it is not easy to be *both just and caring*.

Forgiveness, Justice, and Mercy as Social Virtues

What then is the relationship between forgiveness, justice, and mercy? I suggest three answers to this question. First, the relationship is an intimate one. These three virtues influence each other. What binds them together is the treatment and well-being of others. Secondly, the benefits of cultivating these virtues are enormous in fostering sensitivity to the treatment of others. Thirdly, there are extensive practical difficulties in combining the virtues, and especially in being *simultaneously* forgiving, just, and merciful. Sometimes it may be possible; other times it is not. It is a matter of context, specific detail, relationships, and judgement. Let us explore now the relationship, the benefits, and the difficulties of combining these virtues.

1 Relationship between forgiveness, justice, and mercy

The *relationship* between forgiveness, justice, and mercy is complex. There are some important differences between the virtues. With forgiveness there is a wrongdoer and a person who has been wronged. The wronged person has a right to expect an apology, but this is entirely dependent on the wrongdoer acknowledging personal responsibility for harming another. This acknowledgement frequently does not occur. Despite a willingness to forgive, sometimes we are not given the opportunity to accept an apology, for the apology is never made. Sometimes on these occasions we still can forgive, irrespective of the absence of an apology. With issues of justice there is a person who has a right to fair treatment, and people or organisations who have a moral and legal obligation to treat people without discrimination. Again, the family is a site of many injustices. Mercy differs in that there is a person suffering, but that person has no automatic claim to our assistance. Mercy is a distinctive act of compassion.

What these virtues have in common is that they all affect the ways in which we treat others who are in our care, under our authority, or with whom we must relate. If we have wronged another, we control that person emotionally in withholding our apology. If we refuse to accept a genuine apology, we assert our power to maintain a vivid sense of personal error. Where no apology is made, hurt, bitterness, and pain continues. Few of us can forgive people who have not acknowledged the hurt they have caused, let alone apologised to us. We all have a right to justice, but we are often vulnerable to the way those in authority handle the question of the equal right to fair treatment. Our right to justice does not automatically guarantee that we are treated justly. There are enormous benefits that come from parents asking the forgiveness of children where there is manifest injustice. The benefits include a chance to restore broken relationships, and to start to rebuild a closeness. Wherever forgiveness is not forthcoming, the fault may be because of our recklessness, naivety, selfishness, and conscious mistakes, or it may result from being subject to injustice, prolonged wrongdoing by others, ignorance, and circumstances, and thus we are often at the mercy of others' voluntary compassion.

2 Benefits of forgiveness, justice, and mercy

There are enormous social *benefits* in encouraging people to be forgiving, just, and merciful. People who practise these virtues become sensitive in their treatment of others. In families where the willingness to forgive is a normal occurrence, there is a pardoning of mistakes, a reluctance to bear malice, and what is often a difficult overlooking of others' mistakes. In this context, our essential humanity is manifest —that we all hurt others, do stupid things and make mistakes, but that forgiveness undoes a lot of the potential harm of our mistakes. Where justice prevails, family members can expect to be treated fairly, and to learn the basic principles of distribution, of merit, of unbiased equitable treatment of others, and that, sometimes, mercy overlooks formal principles of rights and expectations.

In a more public context of paid work, or general social relations, there are benefits in having friendships, club members, or work relations that are forgiving, just, and merciful. Certainly justice is the more public virtue. If as an employer I treat two secretaries differently, I must be able to point to some relevant difference that justifies my differential treatment. For example, if I allow one secretary to leave work after lunch, am I being fair to the other secretary? If I am letting the first secretary go off to play golf or have her hair permed I am not acting justly. But if I hear that this secretary has discovered that her adopted daughter has recently had frequent contact with her natural mother, and this is seriously jeopardising their mother–daughter relationship, and her ability to concentrate at work, I might allow her to go to meet the relinquishing mother, informing my secretary of the need to come in earlier in the morning to catch up on her work. I am trying to be *both* just and considerate. If I do not require her to make up the lost time, I will risk my reputation as being fair to all employees. We have a right to equal treatment and to fairness in the work place, so I am likely to explain to both secretaries why the lost hours need to be made up.

In the world of paid work, Equal Employment Opportunity policies and industrial relations awards and requirements are explicit expressions of the need to ensure the just appointment and treatment of employees. Yet, ironically, while Equal Employment policies are meant to ensure fair treatment by being impartial, sometimes particular knowledge of the people involved is necessary in order to be truly fair. Imagine a job situation where two candidates appear to have the same qualifications and experience, and both interview well. Impartiality says we should not know anything about their particular circumstances that might discriminate against them, like their marital status, sexual preference, pregnancy, religion, race, or physical disability. Without this safeguard, positions might tend to go to white, married, physically able men.

But if we know that one of our candidates is the single father of four children who had been on welfare benefits until the youngest was at school, and the other candidate is a man whose partner is in a highly-paid job but who is tired of his financial dependence, would these particular facts influence our decision? More importantly for our present discussion, should they? With globally depressed labour markets and recruitment competitiveness, these questions need to be asked. Given that justice permits relevant reasons for treating people differently, economic need and the ability to support one's family may introduce important particularised considerations into job selections. By allowing candidates to specify what partial knowledge they want exposed, we can prevent coercive intrusions. Candidates might be given the opportunity in the interview to declare any personal factors they would like the selection panel to consider. Public justice procedures may benefit from this extended notion of treating others well.

3 Difficulties in combining forgiveness, justice, and mercy

The third dimension to the relationship between forgiveness, justice, and mercy, relates to the enormous practical *difficulties* in deciding on the appropriateness of applying these virtues. Parents often differ in whether to apply punishment, a pardon, or mercy to a child. These differences can cause havoc between parents, leading to arguments, stressful tensions, siding with or against the child, or violent moments. Decisions about appropriate application of virtues call on our moral judgement and this is where no hard-and-fast guidelines can be set. As outlined in the earlier chapters, morality is an *active process*. It involves agents reacting to different contexts, different moral dilemmas, and different people in different ways. Often this involves almost an intuitive sense of what seems right at the time, together with the need to be accountable for what one decides, and thus to explain one's responses, especially since intuition is only reliably correct in retrospect.

Sometimes it is enormously difficult to forgive others; the personal hurt or disappointment can be totally overwhelming. The woman who is hit by her husband in a cyclical month-on month-off basis, finds it harder and harder to accept his apology as the violence recurs. I am not suggesting we are compelled morally always to forgive. There comes a time in this woman's life when she will refuse to forgive him, for this does not help his problem, and her own self-integrity is at stake and this is more important in a qualitative moral sense than always forgiving.

Similarly, it is very difficult to continually act justly in a family context. How does the ageing business magnate who is redrafting his will take into account the desire to be fair, as well as considering the particular treatment of others? His younger wife has had numerous affairs and an extravagant lifestyle and he has always collected the bill. His oldest son has worked hard with him in the business, has been loyal to his requirements and has maintained friendly relations with his father. The old man is particularly fond of his daughter-in-law and his two grandsons. His own daughter is lazy, arrogant, and inconsiderate, and has treated him instrumentally, as a means to ensuring that she has an easy luxurious lifestyle. She has no intentions of marrying or having children. Yet the old man recognises that she has played a useful role in entertaining some of his important business clients. If she has slept with them as well, this is not his concern. The youngest son left the household as an enraged young writer, angry at the flagrant decadence of his upbringing. Family relationships have been distant and cool, but as his writings become successful, the old man concedes that his youngest son was true to his beliefs in the pursuit of personal integrity, and they have both initiated more contact recently. The father now regrets his harshness, and wants to show mercy to this son.

Justice in a family context requires more than abstract notions of fairness. It must incorporate particular knowledge of family members, and sometimes calls for mercy to be shown. The old man looks back on his life, and weighs *justice with care, merit with his desires, entitlement with his personal biases, compassion with just deserts.* This is no easy task.

Attempts to be simultaneously forgiving, just, and merciful may be impossible in some situations. In other contexts it may be worth striving for. The desire to keep these virtues at the forefront of our moral imaginations and practices keeps us in an active state of trying to treat others well. That is, it requires a moral sensitivity which is crucial to understanding others in complex concrete situations. Morality is grounded in our daily experiences. Our ethics express those connections we have to others in our everyday lives.

8

Caring

Caring is an essential aspect of good families. The deprivation of affectionate care and intimacy has devastating effects on individuals and families. Let me tell you a story about Paul. Paul's mother Jane was fifteen when she gave birth to him. Coming from an unhappy childhood, she had had casual sex since she was thirteen. It used to make her feel just a little bit wanted. Jane did not know who Paul's father was. Her own family would not tolerate Paul's baby cries and forced Jane to leave home. She was a priority case for public housing, especially as a second pregnancy advanced. Jane's new partner saw this relationship as a way to obtain cheap rent. He moved in. Unemployed, he was home a lot. He did not love Jane, beat her regularly, and beat Paul daily. Mother and son both had numerous trips to the hospital casualty department. With two small unhappy babies, Jane was not coping well. Her partner left. Not having a family network to rely on, Jane often left the children home for long periods, huddled together.

Desperate for human warmth, Jane sought the companionship of other men. Numerous men slept over; one man stayed. He used to creep into the bedroom Paul shared with his sister. This man would growl quietly and angrily at Paul, scaring him and threatening him with horrific tales if he dared speak to his mother. This man then slipped into the bed with Paul's sister, sexually abused her, and crept out. She whimpered most of the night. Paul felt sad, but did not know how to respond. Jane suspected what was occurring, but this man actually had a job, and bought her nice clothes, and she did not want this new-found comfort to change, especially when she became pregnant to him. He continued to abuse

Jane's little daughter, terrify her son, and if she raised any complaints with him, he became violent to Jane also.

As Paul became older, he started to articulate his feelings to himself. He hated his new brother's father. He resented his mother for never defending him. He suffered with his sister whose nightly whimpering he had endured for so many years. The night he confronted his mother and told her about his sister, Jane's partner struck him vehemently across the face, cutting his lips. He walked out, never to return, stopping only to whisper a meeting place to his sister. Paul was a street kid from the age of ten, learning how to steal, beg, or cajole enough food to survive. His sister was good to him; there was a real bond of suffering there, and she brought him what food she could.

Paul sat in shopping malls watching people walk by. He would physically flinch every time he saw a young couple in love, a father proudly pushing his child in a pram, a mother with arms of comfort around upset children, a young man hugging his mate in friendly greeting, or an old man putting his arm through an old woman's arm to help her cross the street. He could not recall the last time anyone had touched him with warmth, or anyone except his sister had said anything kind to him. The care in his life was minimal. There was no intimacy. He thought that if love meant sex, why did his sister cry so much? He saw people in love and they looked happy. He did not understand what that might mean.

We all need affectionate care, the intimate closeness of loving relationships. While Paul's story is extreme, it is not rare. People everywhere are deprived of adequate care and yet search for meaningful relationships, for the tenderness of someone who really cares. Popular music screams of the elusiveness of love, reducing it to the passion of sexual desire that is consummated, but the music screams on, 'I can't get no satisfaction, but I try, and I try, and I try'. As family structures alter, as the pace and complexity of life races on, as individualism overshadows our more collective orientations, and as pressures on the welfare state increase while governments look ever more to families to provide care—isolation, loneliness, desolation, and human suffering prevail. It is a reasonable expectation that families should provide affectionate care and intimacy. We need to explore why this does not always occur, and discover how good families can demonstrate these important virtues.

Affectionate Care

I have deliberately combined affection with care to make a specific point. It is possible to care for reasons other than affection. We can care for our neighbour's rottweiler while he is away, by gingerly dropping the food over the back fence, hosing the water bowl from a distance, and running at pace as the huge dog hurtles down the path. But a dog is not a human. We can care for our senile, incontinent parent by paying nursing home fees and visiting the parent monthly. This is a form of care that can be undertaken without real affection being shown. We can care for this parent in our home having some sort of domiciliary service attend our parent a few times a week. We can feed this parent, change the bed linen, and bath the parent, all out of strict duty, without showing any warmth. We can raise our children according to strict inflexible rules and show minimal tenderness to them. We can care for our partner, and even have sexual relations, and yet show no real affection to our lover. Certainly we must question the quality of care all these examples exhibit. The point is that care can be motivated by duty, mutual agreement, social expectations, and parental requirements. This is a minimalist sort of care.

But it is *affectionate care* that I am concerned with, looking first at affection, then at care. When we are affectionate, there are feelings of *fondness* for those for whom we are caring. A soft tenderness pervades our being as we respond to the other with gentleness and with warmth. The *tenderness* is crucial. A ripe soft peach bruises easily if you are rough with it, then it is damaged. A delicate rose is easily crushed and then spoilt. Humans are similar. We are vulnerable, easily crushed, easily bruised, easily damaged. Building on this imagery, the media plays sensitively and instrumentally with some important changes in family structures, like the increased involvement of men in the care of infants. An advertisement showing a man who is physically strong carefully holding a young baby to his masculine chest highlights these themes. Men who are rugged can act with tender warmth to vulnerable children. These are important images to portray in breaking down stereotypes that assume women alone experience feelings of kindness, fondness for others, and a tenderness to those around them.

Expressions of affection

Affection involves two things: an emotional expression and a response. It is an *expression of warmth*, generally exhibited through physical contact, and it is an *attitude of care* that requires a response. First then, affection involves *touch*. In our advertisement the mass media effect would not be the same if a man stood off looking at the baby in a pram. There is a more striking impact when he is holding the infant. From the time a baby is born, touch is inevitable, in bathing the baby, changing nappies, dressing, feeding, and comforting the baby. Traditional notions of western masculinity have excluded men's involvement from this physical arena, both through men's breadwinner role which has meant restricted time with very young children, and through social stereotypes which have decreed that women are associated with realms of nature, the physical, and the emotional, while men are more suited to realms of culture, the mental, and the rational. Both the masculine breadwinner role and strict gender stereotypes are being challenged. As a result, more men are sharing with women in the physical contact of their young children.

Babies who are frequently touched, carried, cuddled, tickled, and massaged do not grow up spoilt and emotionally smothered. They grow up knowing that the giving and receiving of touch is an important part of affirming human attachment. In many traditional cultures infants are continually in close bodily contact, wrapped on to the back or side, even while a mother or a sister works in the field. Children who value touch like to be cuddled, tucked in at night, stroked to sleep, physically comforted when upset, and kissed goodbye. As young people become aware of their own sexuality, their physical contact with family members quite appropriately changes, but the kisses, the hugs, and the arms around the shoulders are a normal part of affectionate families.

Education policies teaching protective behaviour, that children have a right to say 'no' to touch which they feel uncomfortable about are important. Children brought up knowing what is 'good touch' can know when touch exceeds the boundaries of the relationship. For example, a non-custodial father who has a teenage daughter for a weekend may be hurt when she is very distant with him, refusing to sit on the sofa together, but she is probably declaring what forms of physical contact are acceptable to her. Therapy for aggressive children or children like Paul often involves games where touch is essential as part of re-educating children in humanising processes.

Adults too require touch to affirm human warmth—a gesture, a hug, a stroke, a soft hand on the head, a comforting arm, or a soft kiss. Single parents, derelicts, street kids, widowers, widows, prostitutes, and the lonely elderly are groups who often feel the deprivation of affectionate touch. Some nursing homes for the elderly have labrador dogs or rag-doll cats as a source of physical touch for their residents. A common complaint heard by marriage counsellors and family therapists is, 'I know she loves me, but why won't she show me or tell me?' A frequent scene in films is the family gathered around the bedside of a dying family member, waiting for the words or affectionate gestures never uttered or given, but desperately longed for.

Affectionate responses

Secondly, affection involves an attitude that requires action. As we have seen, part of this action involves physical markers. Another part of this action is verbal, words that express warmth, comfort, reassurance, approval, appreciation, and endearment soothe dejected spirits. Other responses are varied. Realising the vulnerability of others, affectionate people act on their *warm-heartedness*. They are considerate, concerned, and show sympathy for those they care about. We need to be interested in our family relationships, to be responsive in ways that are supportive to others' needs, whether this involves a child struggling to find friends at school, a youth who has failed school exams, an unemployed father desperate for work, a bored mother whose children have left home, or a widow who wants to use her deceased spouse's superannuation to travel, rather than to build a small house. This responsiveness calls on *empathy*, the ability to identify with the feelings, thoughts, and attitudes of another person.

To act towards our family members with affectionate sympathy is to have a concern for the consequences of our actions for others. Yelling, screaming, acting vindictively or violently crushes fragile spirits. Yet it is very easy to do. We come home tired, late, irritable, and frustrated, a family member approaches us with their immediate problems, and we lash out. When the cry goes out, 'you don't care about me', what this is saying is that you are not responding in a way that is considerate. You are not identifying with the feelings of the person wanting your care. Generation gaps, cross-cultural relationships, age differences, or value differences all may exacerbate the gap in comprehending the nature of the required care. Bruises heal; scars only fade. We need to respond to family members as fragile, vulnerable beings who need to be shown affection, tenderness, and concerned, responsive sympathy. Emotional bonding and the expression of feelings are important ingredients for good families.

Family care

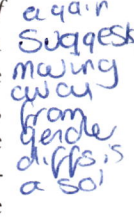

Good families need to pay a lot of attention to the *quality of family care*. When we think of care within a family, we often slip into quick gender differentiations. Men in families are expected to care about their careers, their financial support, and their achievements. Whereas women are expected to care for the physical and emotional needs of those who are dependent, ill, infirm, or disabled. There is a substantial difference in the nature of stereotypical gender-specific care. Caring as an activity is caring out of necessity, or as a duty, like the care of the rottweiler we talked about earlier. I am not saying that a man who is concerned to provide for the economic needs of his family is not caring, or is not affectionately caring, but that men often see caring as an activity that directly reflects individual masculine achievement. In contrast, many women regard caring as a statement of their connections to others, a moral priority that is part of their identity as women. Yet much of this care is taken for granted, viewed as a private matter considered as relevant only to the domestic sphere. In a market economy where relations are primarily instrumental and have an economic price, the sort of care that women have provided historically has been largely undervalued.

Modernity puts so much stress on individual autonomy and on personal freedom, rather than on the care of others, yet there is a deep prevailing longing for a sense of belonging to others. Our yearning is more likely to be fulfilled when we think of the social world as a place where we care for others, instead of seeing our social world as a domain for the pursuit of self-interest. The problem is that we often hear the voice of the rational economic man, who is calculative, emotionally distanced, and his autonomy is defined as independence from others. To recast our social vision, some writers look to the experience of women whose lives traditionally have been associated with care-giving, in order to broaden our understanding of the meaning of caring for others. How we relate to others is the essence of our moral being.

Care of the self and of others

Carol Gilligan is a key cognitive psychologist who is very influential in presenting what she calls a 'care perspective'. In her research she listens to how people experience crises between paying attention to themselves, and responding to the cry of help from others. She suggests that there is something unique in the way many women respond to the conflict between *caring for their selves* and *caring for others*. Examples of this conflict between self and other include: a woman considering an unwanted pregnancy, having to weigh up her right to reproductive freedom and responsibility, versus the foetus' right to life; a woman's readiness to have a desired pregnancy and the support network available; a woman's desire or financial need to work, and her family's need for her care.

Gilligan traces typical stages women seem to go through in coming to grips with this conflict between self and others.

8 Caring   127

To trace these stages, let us take Sally, a single mother who has just left a destructive relationship. Rather than remaining in a dysfunctional unit, this woman sets out to re-establish her life in a positive way.

1. Initially, there is a concern just with *self-survival*, as well as feeling powerless, disconnected, and lonely. Basic survival is the prime concern.

2. Survival alone seems insufficient, even selfish, so Sally starts to consider the possibility of a *concern for herself* as well as for her young children. She is receiving welfare, is in a rent-subsidised house, and she starts to think how she will cope.

3. Sally is confused. She is accustomed to associating *feminine moral goodness* with the *care of dependants*. She really wants to return to study to become more qualified and to get a good job, but childcare is a problem, and she thinks she might not be able to combine her aims to be a good mother and to study well. Besides, her ageing parents are becoming more frail, and her brother expects her to attend to their many needs.

4. She talks with friends who are studying and she realises she does not have to be self-sacrificial to be a good mother, that she can *include her own needs* within her moral judgement. She decides she will study and that others can care for her children for a while. She forms a community babysitting group.

5. Her whole way of approaching dilemmas that concern her self and others has changed. She realises that to think of care she must be *honest to her own needs as well as to others*, and that this extension of the parameters of care alters her appreciation of what constitutes care. She enrols in her studies and starts reading. The intellectual demands and break away from her children stimulate her, and give her renewed energy to care for her children and parents, and to take her share in the baby-sitting group.

6. Sally now has a transformed understanding of relationships. She sees the interconnections between herself and those she cares for in her daily life as being an integral

part of her moral judgements. *Care of selves-in-relations* becomes her self-chosen moral principle. Decisions she needs to make now involve considerations of herself and others.

These stages are not unique to women. They reveal an approach to care typical for those who have cared for others at the expense of themselves, then, who through life experiences, adopt a broader understanding of care that includes *both* the self and others.

Another contrasting view of care concerns the reasons why some people see *care of the self* to be primary, and why others feel committed to include the *care of others as well* as of the self. Gilligan contrasts two perspectives.

- An assertive sense of self is defined through an emotional distancing from others, and bases itself on a *morality of rights*. The moral dilemma at stake is the balance of claims to rights between separate self-assertive beings. *Individual autonomy* defines this perspective.

- A self defined through connections to others bases itself on a *morality of responsibilities*. Morality is taken to be a problem of inclusion of those requiring care. *Interdependence* characterises the responsibilities perspective.

In the first perspective, autonomy refers more to an individualist self rather than the positive sense of autonomous individuality I advocated in Chapter 3. The second perspective looks towards an idea of interdependence which I develop in Chapter 10. Both perspectives combine a notion of rights and responsibilities to be explained in Chapter 11.

Generally speaking, men's practical life situations have led them to adopt a self-assertive rights perspective, whereas women's practical experience as reproducers or as nurturers have encouraged a perspective of responsibility and care. These are generalisations: we all know ruthless self-interested women, and compassionate sensitive men. But, given that it is still women who usually are the prime parents, and are numerically dominant in service-caring employment like nursing, childcare, early childhood education or social welfare, there appear to be unique features about women's care. I want to draw attention to two features of care—the *unique attentiveness*, and the *particularity of care*.

1 Caring attentiveness

Like affection, caring involves emotions and responses. If we say we care for our child, we do not just feel warm and fuzzy towards this person; we act on our feelings. Being concerned for this child, we respond to their sense of wavering wellbeing because it matters to us in an intensely personal way. We do not sit around theorising about ideal ways to handle discipline problems of a child who hates school, another who is experimenting with drugs and under-aged heavy drinking, another contemplating sex before the age of consent, and another who is depressed and talking about suicide. When we grapple with these issues, it is at a specific engaged level of thought.

Sara Ruddick, writer on 'maternal thinking', suggests that this sort of thinking arises out of specific social practices that are responses to particular people who require *preservatory care*. This care involves a unity of emotion, reflection, and judgement. We care emotionally about someone, reflect on alternative ways of relating to or treating them, and choose appropriate responses. Sometimes we act inappropriately, we all make mistakes, that is part of being human. Ruddick suggests that at the foundation of this unique thought is an attitude she calls 'holding' which involves *conserving the fragile*. It recognises the profound unpredictability of much of life. It is an intellectual activity directed towards everyday moments when we are attending to others and imaginatively caring, trying to see what the other person is really going through.

Learning how to hold the fragile usually arises from the specific attentiveness necessary for childcare, where a newborn baby is checked every few moments, a toddler is watched closely to prevent him or her from running on the road, the train track, or by the river, an adolescent is watched as identity changes may be confusing, or a young adult facing unemployment after graduation is watched carefully for lagging spirits. While maternal thought usually arises from caring for children, the biological aspects are less significant. 'Maternal' is a social category. You can be maternal to adoptive children, foster children, friends, students, patients, clients, parishioners, or even to your own mother. This *nurturing, attentive holding of the fragile* is part of the thought process and moral construction of anyone engaged in the regular care of others.

Yet much of our everyday family life works against attentive care. There is an intensity of family emotions that often range over the full gamut of love, hatred, despair, unrealistic expectations, jealousy, pride, arrogance, and stubbornness. These emotions flow into the daily wear and tear of tiring, arduous, boring mundanities, verbal jibes, conflict of interests, and the clamour and egoism of households that are part and parcel of much of life. Familial attentiveness recognises the inevitable ups and downs of family life, but rectifies some of these daily hassles just by constantly trying to 'hold' fragile beings.

2 Particularity of care

The second dimension of care is its *particularity*. It is particular people we care for—a lover dying of AIDS, a retrenched de facto husband, a son with a broken leg, or a daughter repeating exams. Attentive care involves judgements that draw on our experiential basis of knowledge. We need specific knowledge of the person we are caring for in order to meet adequately their particular, concrete needs. Without this knowledge we are limited in our receptivity to their needs. Particular people require particular responses. The more we know about someone, the more likely we are to respond with a form of affectionate care that is truly considerate.

We quickly learn that a baby cries from hunger, discomfort, pain, boredom, tiredness, or fear. Our caring responses have to be sensitive to the different cues, the different types of crying, screaming, whimpering, or sulking. Communication aids the process with older children, 'what's wrong dear?' being the starting point. Often we make mistakes in our responses. A phone message for my husband might request that he goes out tonight after work. I might decide that he is too tired and not tell him until it is too late. He might be cross at my withholding of the message, and my care fails to fulfil the goodwill intended. So even careful judgements about people we know exceptionally well do not always accurately reflect specific requirements.

To summarise, women's historical association with attentive, particularised care of vulnerable others has much to teach us all about how to respond caringly to others. Yet this affectionate care is not an achievement for all women, let alone all mothers. The daily struggle of many households keeps family units at a mere survival level, not allowing the flourishing of the sorts of care that take into account the needs of all members of the family unit. Furthermore, some men might recognise this account of affectionate care as more reflective of their caring relationships. The point is that when *ethical caring* sees a direct connection between the *self and others*, where there is a real commitment to respond with affectionate, tender responsiveness to those people we live with, then we affirm the moral dimension of the activity of caring for others. This is as important for men as it is for women.

Intimacy

Affectionate care sets up the dynamics for creating intimate families. A man has had a tough day at work. He comes home to be greeted by a warm smile, a cup of tea, and happy children playing. A woman has worked the night hospital shift, and comes home to a hot breakfast prepared by her older children, and her husband has the younger children ready for school, lunches packed. The executive couple cruise by the take-aways, select a dish, and settle down by the fire, beer in one hand, Indian curry in the other. A child comes home after being teased all day at school about his new haircut, irritable with his school friends and teachers, and instantly throws off his bad mood as he walks into the kitchen and smells freshly baked cookies his Gran has made. Are these examples just for the television? Why do we accuse them of excessive romanticism? What each example shares is a milieu of intimacy, an intimacy that should not be mocked, just because it is rare. We can explain this intimacy at three levels.

1 General warmth

At a general level, intimacy creates *a feeling of warmth*. The atmosphere is informal, snug, and cosy, and what we often respond to is the mere familiarity of it all. The child comes home from school, throws the school bag down, gets a glass of milk and something to eat, and plonks down in front of the television for a while before going out to play. A simple pattern, but a positive response to informal familiarity. The teenage girl likes her room in a mess; it is a sign of feeling comfortable with her possessions and she sits curled up with her best friend chatting for hours. Friends call over unannounced and you spontaneously invite them for dinner. The food is simple, the setting informal, around the kitchen table, or on cushions around a coffee table, and there is a cosy intimacy.

2 Cherished moments

The second level of intimacy involves *things or moments we really cherish*. They are deeply personal things, often very private, and involving confidentiality. Landmarks shared in our maturation come into this sphere—a birth, a christening, a confirmation, a bar mitzvah, a graduation, the loss of virginity, wedding anniversaries, receiving an antique photo of a relative, or an old silver locket from a grandmother. It includes the look in a father's eye as he walks down the aisle with his daughter on her wedding day. It is the look of a new parent watching a partner give birth to their child. It is the look in a lover's eye the first time those famous words, 'I love you' are uttered.

3 Deep intimacy

The third level of intimacy involves *a deep understanding of others*. Here there is a real closeness, an intense sense of connectedness to the other. This is a profound, thorough intimacy that relates to the essential core of our need to be part of an intimate sphere. It is the sort of intimacy partners in love hope to achieve with each other. This sort of intimacy requires meaningful communication to ascertain what we share in common, and what affirms our bond. As Charles Taylor, political philosopher, puts it, if music is one dimension of this bond, listening to Mozart with an intimate partner is quite different from listening to Mozart alone.

To be able to share at this deep level needs constant work and negotiation of busy schedules to make time to be intimate. Where there is a partner, regular time needs to be set aside for a drink and a chat that goes beyond mundanities, the children's problems, work difficulties, or household maintenance. This form of intimacy needs to reach to the core of each partner's being, to know each other's goals, fears, and desires. In my marriage, there has rarely been a day where some time has not been snatched, away from the children, daily tasks, or work life to sit together, sometimes with music, a coffee, or wine, and during this time, we talk and talk. *Intimacy matters.* It provides a richness for loving relations which we explore in the next chapter.

Caring Communities

Structures for affectionate care and intimacy grow out of the family. We expect families to include in this care disabled, ill, and dependent relatives. The type of care provided changes over the life-cycle. Independent children who leave home with a partner, may, if they are part of a close family, live close to the neighbourhood of the parent unit. Where many family units choose to live near by, they are likely to care for each other in times of crises, like illness, financial troubles, employment difficulties, or sudden death. This variant of the extended family structure exists predominantly in community-oriented cultures, in close-knit working-class areas, in rural regions, and in certain ethnic communities living in individualistic cultures.

Even in eastern cultures the changes in social values, and the importance placed on participation in the paid workforce, are altering traditional care in similar ways to western individualist societies. Now it is more typical for one's primary family members to be divorced, form new blended families with step-parents and stepchildren, or to avoid marriage through de facto relations, single parenthood, same sex coupling, single careerist celibacy, or voluntary childlessness. There are different challenges, tasks, and problems in these lifestyle patterns and needs for care, compared with traditional family forms. We need to work on ways that might improve these patterns of care so that *appropriate care* is adapted, for social change often occurs rapidly without us understanding what is happening.

While these changes in family structures have increased personal freedom and choice, they have also broken down the life-cycle of care, where family members could *expect care* from other family members when it was needed, and where family members would provide the necessary care. I am not romanticising old family forms. In traditional families, there was a narrow gender division of labour, as well as child abuse, domestic violence, women with more children than they had the energy, time, or money for, and men whose wages did not adequately support their families. My point is simply that social problems emerge when care can no longer be taken for granted from families. It is characteristic of a strong family that family members turn to one another for help in times of difficulty, whether this is a partner's infidelity, children's behavioural problems, strains in relationships, economic distress, medical problems, prevailing violence, or abuse contributing to intimidation, coercion, threats, violence, sexual control, or death. Many people do not belong to strong, reliable family networks.

As family bonds weaken, many people are increasingly reliant on the state for caring. Most of us can accept institutionalised care for those requiring intensive or specialised care, like the severely disabled, the insane, and the senile. After that we fall into some social policy dilemmas. Most of us accept that public care-giving service is a social right that accrues to citizens of a social welfare state. But what sort of public care do we want? The sort of affectionate care we described earlier relies on a close knowledge of the person requiring care. Instead, public care is often a market-oriented version of care, dominated by professional educators, advisers, social workers, and consultants. Certainly the nursing profession values touch, yet the idea of public service generally is one that is distanced from particularised attentive care. For some people there is no choice. Some care is better than no care, regardless of where it comes from. The increasing demands on religious, charitable, and community welfare services testify both to the weakening of traditional forms of family and social care, and to the escalating need for an expansion of public care-giving services.

Rather than a formal, cold, public care, community care is *morally preferable* in that the social responsibility to care emanates from a direct, personal involvement with people. When it is care and attentiveness that is needed, we prefer to receive this from someone we know, and preferably know well. In contexts where local community bonds are relatively weak, where the population is highly mobile, and where mothers and grandmothers are in the workforce, people have less time, energy, and commitment to be with families. But when we talk about community care, who is the community? Partners are equally likely to care for an elderly, infirm, or dying partner. Men who have never married or are divorced and return to the family home often care for elderly parents. In other situations mothers, grandmothers, daughters, and daughters-in-law are the main care-givers. Most often women have to cope with the deficiencies of the welfare state, a problem when they are trying to gain increased command over their own economic independence. There is a danger in community care being overly reliant on traditional roles of women as natural carers, without acknowledging the unpaid nature of much of this care, the time and energy expended, and the socially necessary contribution care makes. Who cares for the carers?

Affectionate care and intimacy are not virtues exclusive to women. Protection, nurture, tenderness, and species integration are not instinctual to femininity. If more women are caring, it is due to their care of children in particular, and their commitment to care. As such, these are learned faculties, *human capacities* open to all who are *receptive to the needs of others.* Parents able to communicate as affectionate carers convey a sense of authentic nurture which lays the foundation for future generations of caring adults. It is crucial for men to participate in childcare and to develop their nurturing capacities. This involvement requires significant social structural changes. Men need to relinquish some of the power of their favoured public positions. Women need to relinquish total control over household matters. Policies need to reform the world in terms of good childcare and flexible work arrangements that are responsive to human needs, not just market demands. Employers need to encourage caring work relationships. Ethical caring then translates into the social, civic, and public realms.

9

Loving Friendship

The good of the family is its well-being. Intrinsic to this well-being is knowing that others in our families:

- are attached to us
- have affection for us
- delight in our presence
- enjoy being with us
- take pleasure in our company
- show fond warmth toward us.

Knowing that others have a strong attachment to us reassures us that we are loved. If we are deprived of love, we feel insecure, and unsure of ourselves in relation to others, especially those for whom we have some fond feelings. Whatever complaints or regrets I may have about the restrictiveness of much of my upbringing, I am immensely grateful that I grew up never having to question whether I was a wanted child. In my father's words, I am his 'favourite fifth child'. I was a loved child who was carried about frequently by my two eldest sisters, as well as by my mother, and by Javanese villagers, and house-helpers. In photos of me as a baby, and as a little girl, I am in the centre of many people who are expressing their love for me. This is a precious heritage of security that I take into my adult life.

Clearly, love is not the dominant emotion or motivation for behaviour in many families. Hatred, bitterness, resentment, jealousy, and anger often lie parallel to loving relationships, or sometimes go in the opposite direction. Domestic violence, child sexual abuse, emotional and physical abuse of the elderly, intense discord, rebellious youth, high levels of divorce, messy custody arrangements, awkward step-relations, and familial discontent are ample evidence that loving relationships in families are not the norm. Indeed, outside of the military, the family is the most physically violent group we are likely to encounter. We are more likely to be beaten, raped, or murdered by our immediate family, relatives, or close friends than by a stranger. This family violence often occurs after a festivity like Christmas, when frenetic emotions, long-held grudges, debts, and excessive alcohol contribute to volatile eruptions. Yet most of us search for love, and we usually begin our search in our families.

I have deliberately combined love and friendship in this chapter for quite specific reasons. I want to make three main points.

1. There are many types of loving relations, and most of us experience them all at different stages of our lives.
2. The combination of love and friendship is unique, and more attention needs to be directed at this combination, in terms of relationships between partners, between siblings, and between parents and children.
3. Strengthening loving friendships within families creates a basis for a strong version of human solidarity that has a positive influence on our social relationships and commitments to general social tasks.

Love

What is love? It is an elusive mystery that most of us spend a lot of time and energy searching for. Popular music never stops trying to define it. Glossy magazines continually write about it. Romance fiction is a burgeoning industry. Love relations are an integral part of television soapies. Media images play on the search for love, the intensity of passion, the fulfilment of desire, the deep longing for attachment. The allure surrounding passionate desire is used to try to sell perfume, lingerie, cars, and holidays.

Not all cultures are preoccupied with love. Many cultures look for different forms, such as beauty, character, health, and good child-bearing hips as assets in intimate relationships. In these cultures, affection comes as a product of the union, seen as a process resulting from living together and of co-operating in many activities, particularly the rearing of children, so that with time you become fond of your partner. Marriage thus is viewed as an alliance between two groups of kin who have a common interest in the offspring of the union, who then become kin to both groups. This alliance provides an important basis for a valued social network.

In contrast, the west gives precedence to individual choice and self-fulfilment, and sees love very much as an individual response to another. Many people associate love solely with emotions and strong feelings. The classic accusation, 'you don't really love me, if you did you wouldn't be so selfish' makes sense. It is not that we won't be selfish at times, but that *love* is more than an emotional state, it is an *active virtue*. It must keep proving itself to be realised as true. It must keep *demonstrating its potency*, so that the object of love is in no doubt that s/he is being loved. When love is seen just as a self-satisfying emotion, the glib message that 'I love you' can mean something like 'you give me a buzz', or 'you turn me on', but equally, when the buzz fades, the love disappears. We have used the other just for some personal pleasure or self-satisfaction.

There are many different sorts of love, and the term is used very loosely. If I said 'I love chocolate, I love big long-haired dogs, I love good claret, I love the colour blue, I love my friends, I love my kids, and I love my husband', I would not want you to think that the same meaning of love was applied to all these examples. We have different love relations with different people. We respond differently to different objects of love. This is important to grasp, for many people have been reluctant to admit to love apart from erotic or romantic relations. I want to use and extend the psychologist Steve Duck's sixfold categorisation. He uses the Greek terms:

1. *Eros*—sexual love
2. *Ludus*—game-playing love
3. *Storge*—friendship love
4. *Pragma*—logical love

5. *Mania*—dependent love
6. *Agape*—altruistic love.

1 *Eros*—sexual love

To understand this form of erotic, sexual love, we need to go back to Greek mythology. Eros, the Greek god of love, is regarded as the son of Aphrodite, goddess of sexual love and the 'higher' love of beauty, and the son, controversially, of Zeus, Hermes, or Ares. Eros represents the force of irresistible attraction between two people, the physically magnetic force which pulls people together to lavish and to be lavished with sensual delights and physical pleasures of a highly sexual nature. Eros plays on being the god of sexual desire. He too has an object of love.

Psyche is a princess of such remarkable beauty that Aphrodite herself is jealous of her. Aphrodite instructs Eros to punish Psyche. Instead, he visits her regularly at night, keeping his face hidden. Her sisters laugh at her and say that any man who hides his face must be a monster. One night, overcome by curiosity, she lights a lamp and sees his charm, but a drop of oil falls on his shoulder and he vanishes. After many ordeals from Aphrodite's anger, Eros and Psyche (soul) marry, and Psyche is granted immortality. In this story we get a wonderful *union of sexual desire and soul*, providing depth of love. Love and sex are fused, and sex confirms the love relationship.

In later Hellenic times, Eros is represented as a slightly rebellious winged youth armed with bow and arrows whose barb stirs the fires of passion. Eros is also associated with romantic love, a passionate affection for another that stirs strong emotions of ecstasy, excitement, and exhilaration in desire to be together. Romantic love is profoundly tender, and intense. Eros is a driving force.

Plato presents *eros* as the driving power of life which propels life towards the union with the true and the good. In the *Phaedrus*, he distinguishes between an unreasonable eros, blinded by desires directed exclusively to beautiful bodies and momentary physical possession, and a reasonable eros, aroused by the fact that what is loved in the other person is the idea of beauty, and the whole of self. With this form of eros, the soul is present in the erotic act, a fusion of reason and passion, soul and sex. While two become as one, the individuality of the person is crucial, otherwise partners would be quite interchangeable.

2 *Ludus*—game-playing love

Game-playing love is not too serious. Its motivation is fun, so it is light-hearted and flirtatious. Examples of this sort of love are a good night on the town with a group of close friends, dancing together, laughing together, perhaps touching playfully. A bonfire on the beach is lit, and couples frolic joyfully about. A couple lie in bed after a spa together, giggling in delight. A more contentious dimension to this form of love is recreational sex which seems to fit into this category and which is a form of flirtatious play. AIDS and STDs are changing some people's sexual game-playing patterns and most people still want sex to be accompanied by affection, if not the depth-of-soul companionship of Eros and Psyche.

3 *Storge*—friendship love

Friendship love is based not on sexual passion, but on caring for another person with whom you share interests. It grows with a respect and a concern for the other. The goodness of friendships lie in the common actions and meanings shared between close friends. It is most comprehensive between two lovers whose sexual involvement includes friendship. (Friendship love is the focus of the latter part of this chapter, so it will be developed fully there.)

4 *Pragma*—logical love

Pragmatic love is based on the belief that the relationship has to work. It is unromantic, realistic, and takes into account the other's background, attitudes, religion, and politics. It is judged by its practical consequences, such as with arranged marriages, adopted children, foster children, and step-relations. In all these situations, you often know little about the person involved, but you do know that a real effort must be made to make the relationships work. Another dimension to this pragmatic love exists in cultures dominated by individual self-fulfilment, where both partners communicate only to the extent that prime erotic claims are fulfilled. When there is no satisfaction, when age, habit, over-familiarity, or boredom set in, the pragmatics of the relationship break down. One partner is dismissed or chooses to leave. In other relationships, the partners stay together, 'for the sake of the children'.

5 *Mania*—dependent love

In dependent love one's needs are fulfilled by the other. It is easy to understand this in terms of a child's love for a parent. The child is anxious and uncertain, and the child's needs for food, clothing, and emotional security are taken care of. It also manifests itself when intense psychological needs of adults have been denied in the past and sought for in a lover. A man whose mother died in childbirth and who hates his stepmother looks for a woman with strong motherly, nurturant qualities. A young woman whose father has always been dismissive towards her starts to date a man twice her age.

What often accompanies these relationships is an extreme possessiveness, a domination, an unbalanced dependence, or a manipulation of the other for self-satisfaction. These forms of dependency are not healthy, but adult dependent love is not always negative. It is valuable when it involves mutual dependency, so that one partner can be wholly dependent on the other for a short period of tiredness, illness, or financial need, knowing that in another situation this will be reciprocated.

6 *Agape*—altruistic love

Altruistic love is motivated by an unselfish concern for the well-being of others. It is a real giving of oneself, an investment of one's energies in caring for others. This love is compassionate, thoughtful, considerate, humble, forgives readily, protects, and trusts. Its satisfaction is derived from the meaning gained from nurturing someone else. As we saw in the previous chapter, this sort of care requires particularised knowledge of the person. Theologian Paul Tillich adds a useful explanation to altruistic love. He writes that this form of love cuts through the separation of equals and unequals, of sympathy and antipathy, of friendship and indifference, of desire and disgust, that is, it conquers some of the ambiguities of love and the object of love. It is what motivates people to work with drug addicts, juvenile delinquents, alcoholics, the homeless, the suicidal, the depressed unemployed, the starving, and the unlovely.

Loving relationships

To summarise these six categorisations of love, good families, where there is a couple, will generally exhibit a healthy balance of these six forms of love at different stages of their lives and in different circumstances. In single-headed families, there may be minimal or no opportunity for *erotic love*, but the other forms of love can still exist. Anyway, most of us enjoy the delights of erotic, sexual pleasure. Those who choose to live without sexual intimacy because they value something else more highly, such as a commitment to a religious ideal, channel affective needs into a vocation, but there is an escalating questioning regarding many branches of the Church's harsh stance towards enforced celibacy.

There are ample opportunities in families for *game-playing love*. Yet despite better work conditions, many of us work too hard, for too many hours, and we lose the joys of simple, not too serious play. *Friendship love* is crucial for good families. It cements shared bonds and a commitment to maintain common interests. Family relationships often falter, and considerations of *pragmatic love* are thrust upon us. Knowing that the relationships must work for all sorts of reasons, we approach these relationships from a practical, logical angle. We all have unfulfilled needs and look for others to satisfy us. *Dependent love* is a feature of family lives, problematic when it is not reciprocated. *Altruistic love* is a necessary antidote to self-motivated desires.

We have achieved our first aim, to show that there are many types of loving relationships. Most of us will experience all of them at some stage in our lives. Our next aim is to understand more about the unique combination of love and friendship, particularly as it emerges in families—between partners, between siblings, and between parents and children. We have looked at love, and before we look at love and friendship, we need to understand more about friendship.

Friendship

Friendships are important, for we are social beings. Yet there are times when we all need to be by ourselves. We may need to work through some ideas, reflect, and meditate, or just escape from the pressures of pacy lifestyles. This self-chosen solitariness is not loneliness. Loneliness is the discrepancy between one's desired and achieved levels of social relations. It is being alone when we would rather be with someone. It is feeling socially and emotionally isolated, unattached, estranged, or dislocated. The reasons for loneliness differ. For some it might stem from an early rejection in the family, or an intense shyness, or feelings of personal inadequacy, or a broken relationship, a separation, a divorce, a death of one's spouse or another family member. It may come as a result of frequent relocations, where one has just started to put down roots, and these are pulled up abruptly. Some people find it difficult to make new friends as they get older.

Lillian Rubin in her book *Just Friends* writes that when friends are described as 'like family', this suggests something about the importance of the relationship, that there is an intensity of connection, a rich sense of belonging, a closeness, an attachment, an affinity, and a real rapport with those we know well, are on good terms with, and share a lot in common with. It is true that we often value friends in contrast to family members because, as Rubin puts it, 'they accept me for who I am', that is, they have chosen to be friends with me in a way family members thrown together have no choice. We have heard the phrase 'a friend is closer than a brother'. Again, we have the idea that there is no choice regarding kin, and many of us are not close to some of our kin. But a friend is self-chosen; there is something special about the person chosen.

Modern society fragments much of life, and the disruption to families who frequently move suburbs, states, or countries in search of employment or promotion, separates family members, making the search for friendships more urgent, and often more difficult. It is normal to shed friends as we move in and out of school classes, new jobs, new partners, and in-laws. But how many of us have friends we have gone to school with, shared our childhood and adolescent dreams and fears with, whispered our first love to, puffed our first cigarette with, debated sex, graduated, exchanged tales about love desired and fulfilled, or love sought for and lost? And how many of these friends have we continued to have meaningful contact with through our adult single life, or as we marry, have children, divorce, repartner, have more children and affairs, try celibacy, and new jobs, and share the pain and joys of bringing up children? I think few of us have friends we have had this sort of continuity with, where we can pick up where we left off, no matter how many years gap between our last contact, and where a host of unspoken cues hover, mutually understood.

Most of us have different sorts of friends. Some friends help us to relax; with other friends we have more serious discussions on the big issues of life. We seek out some friends when we are sad and in need of comfort, or when tragedy strikes and we need others to lean on for emotional support. Other friends share our love for hiking, flower arrangement, silent movies, playing tennis, or fishing. Some friends are better friends because we share so much in common with them. Our relationship is easy, we are quite comfortable to just be ourselves, and we have shared memorable moments with them.

Quality of friendship

We can judge the *quality of friendship* by the degree to which friends *care for each other.* Aristotle is very clear on this. 'Without friends', he writes, 'no one would choose to live'. Friends are so important to our well-being. 'The man who is to be happy will therefore need virtuous friends.' Thus, 'we define a friend as one who wishes and does what is good, or seems so, for the sake of his friend'. This involves a mutual goodwill, but it is more than this, for we can have goodwill toward people we do not know well—the baker or the butcher. The goodwill we are talking about here is based on friendship. Aristotle writes some things about friendship that appear astonishing to the modern person. Because 'friendship requires time and familiarity', what contributes to friendship is, in Aristotle's view, a similarity of age, a common upbringing, an equality, much sharing in discussion and thought, and the common property that comes from living together or is dependent on community. Where these contributions to friendship exist, this familiarity lays the foundation for friendships within families.

This sort of friendship clearly requires active working, with duties towards friends, like keeping promises, acting fairly, telling the truth, keeping confidences, and showing gratitude. A person who is a good friend will take care not to violate duties of friendship. Indeed, failure to fulfil duties may justify ending the friendship. Neglect of friendship, failing to phone, to write, to visit, or to invite each other out leads to a petering out of the bond. So does a betrayal of confidence, or an intrusion into what someone considers to be private. Friendship involves a concern for the well-being of our friends. When we cease to be concerned with the good, our friendship ceases to be meaningful. Given that the well-being of our families is the focus of this book, I shall show how this well-being involves a unique blend of familial love and familial friendship.

Love and Friendship

The potential combination of love and friendship in families is unique, and more attention to this combination is needed, for clearly many families do not express loving friendships. But, first, a word about this combination. It is true that one of the distinct differences between family and friends is that, aside from a partner, we do not choose our children, our parents, our siblings, aunts, uncles, cousins, step-relations, grandparents, or in-laws, whereas our friends are self-chosen.

Because of this distinction between natural and self-chosen relationships, many of us have not viewed our family as potential friends. Another reason is the unequal power relations that often emerge in families between spouses, between older and younger siblings, between siblings of the opposite sex, between the children of a stepfather and the children of a stepmother in a blended family, and between this couple's new children.

What power relations do is to set up hierarchies that preclude friendships being formed. Generally, close friendships do not form between a pupil and a headmaster, between a clerk and a bank manager, or between a surgeon and a patient. There are practical and professional reasons why this does not occur, particularly to avoid unfair biases. Hierarchies and power differentials ensure that close comradeship does not result. As we have noted, friendships are more likely to occur amongst people of equal standing who share similar interests. If friendships are to develop within loving family relations, inflexible hierarchies of power, status, and control need to be broken down. Let us explore the possibilities of loving friendships developing between partners, siblings, and parents and children.

1 Love and friendship between partners

In families where there are partners living together, we would expect there to be a combination of love and friendship with these partners, but this does not always happen. When a couple start dating, there is usually a mixture of physical attraction and personality factors. The couple relate to each other for who they are—warm, kind, gregarious, humorous, or interesting people who are mutually attracted. In the early days of the relationship, there is often a sincere attempt to discover shared interests that are an intrinsic part of friendship. The question of compatibility is crucial, that is, the capability of living together in reasonable harmony, evaluated according to general temperament, values, and attitudes. Many couples now choose to cohabit for varying reasons—as a utilitarian arrangement in that it is cheaper living in one place, as a trial marriage, as a prelude to marriage, or as an alternative to marriage. Other partners marry and then live together. There is a slow trend among career-oriented partners, creative writers, or artists, who are committed to each other, toward maintaining separate residences.

So why do we not always see the combination of love and friendship between partners? I suggest that what often happens is the over-emphasis of the erotic to the detriment of *affectionate bonding*, and thus little scope is given to the development of a rich friendship. The lovers are filled with mutual passionate desire, there is a strong physical attraction, an urgent need for sexual union, and sex informed by the mutual love heightens sexuality. There is the romance of flowers, dinners together, gifts exchanged, and the newness of the moment, where each new event signifies a symbolic milestone. What then happens in many relationships is that there is insufficient time and energy put into developing *companionship*, where both partners are interested in each other, enjoy each other's company, have shared common interests, including other friends in common, and spend time talking to each other, doing activities together, and sharing life experiences, desires, hopes, and fears. Consequently, deep meaningful friendships do not develop.

There are a number of reasons for this. There are traditional gender explanations. Where a man sees his role in traditional terms as an authority figure and the head of a household, he is likely to view his partner as someone whom he can control, dominate, and possess. He may be emotionally dependent on this woman, but he is not likely to view her as his friend. Similarly, where a woman sees her role as a socialiser of children, a nurturer, and domestic labourer who is subordinate to her male partner, she is not likely to view him as her friend. There are other gender explanations.

Male friendships with other men usually pivot around common activities like playing sport together, fixing a car together, building a house together, or drinking together. Female friendships are characterised typically by a sharing of emotional intimacies, and a mutual support network for nurturing children. Spousal jealousy over cross-sex friendships often means that some partners have had little practice in relating well to peers of a different sex. Women who have men friends, and men who have women friends, are more likely to be comfortable in developing a close friendship with their partners. With some of these men and women, sexual difference is an irrelevant dimension to their friendship. With others, it heightens the interest in the friendship, with a mutual consciousness of sexual identity, and of the pleasures of sensual differences.

There are other features of modern social life that also work against partners developing loving friendships. Many households require two incomes; partners work long hours and come home tired. There are usually household chores to do and children often preoccupy adults' free time at home. The television, when used as a leisure pursuit, does not encourage the dialogue that is crucial to good communication. Many partners do go out together, but go to paid amusements where there is little time for talking intimately. Disillusionment, fading passion, boredom, and restlessness often sets in. The pace and complexity of life works against the requirements of friendship—time and motivation to pursue shared interests and ideas.

In contrast, couples who are aware of the potential infringement of daily demands, yet who want to *merge their love and friendship*, ensure that they regularly spend quality time with each other. Despite the pace of life, and demands of work, children, or other people, they find time that can be regularly spent affirming their love through their friendship. When we are in love, we see the world not only through our own eyes, but through the eyes of the person we love. This means we have an openness to their perceptions, we want to be an instrument of their happiness. This is a *creative exercise* that broadens our horizons. It involves working at knowing who our partner really is. It does not endanger individuality, rather it calls for a mutual revelation of differences. Time, dialogue, and openness are essential to a mutual revelation of selves.

The excitement between persons who love each other is based on sharing. It is this loss of sharing that is one of the chief causes of grief with a bereaved partner. Frequent quick remarriages or repartnering can be explained not in terms of disrespect for the death of the beloved, but by the longing for reconnection with another which grows out of the intensity of the loss. Where partners are lovers and friends, there is a desire for the lovers to be together, a centrality of passion, an intense identification with each other, a validation of one another's uniqueness, and an affectionate bonding that underlies mutual care and loyalty. While length of time together does not always confirm this sort of deep relationship, older people who can look back on their adult lives as a wonderful partnership of loving friendship have much to rejoice in.

2 Love and friendship between siblings

Whether siblings and step-siblings develop loving friendships or not depends on a number of factors. Partners who prize their friendship, or who desperately long for it, or who after separation or death mourn the loss of this sharing, are likely to encourage their children to be friends. Other factors come into play, like the age difference between siblings, the sex of siblings, how much they have been thrown together through travel, illness, financial hardship, a traumatic divorce of their parents, or custody battles, as well as personality factors, and shared interests.

For most of my childhood and adolescence I shared a bedroom with my sister who is two years younger. Because of the age similarity, we were at the same primary and then secondary school. We walked or rode bikes to school together, shared similar interests in reading books, playing sport, and swimming. We chatted and giggled together most nights. Although our interests have diverged as adults, we shared a lot of common experiences together which laid the basis for a bond of familiarity. When I was a child, there was not the same effort, opportunity, or encouragement to develop friendships with my older siblings, and there were significant generation differences. My younger sister and I were teenagers in the late 1960s and early 1970s, eras of experimentation, questioning, and rejection of status quo values and practices, including those relating to traditional families. My four older siblings have lived in other states or countries most of my adult life. The friendships I do have with them are friendships developed primarily as adults, and these vary in depth.

Yet because of their freely chosen nature, these friendships permit new discoveries of adult affection. I compare my childhood with the life of my own three children.

There is five years difference between the oldest and the youngest. Consequently, they face an awareness of similar generational issues—the need for educational qualifications, the difficulties of obtaining employment, a prevailing materialistic ethos existing alongside global, ecological crises. They live in an information and technology saturated world, where appearance and brand name grant them peer credibility. They have travelled abroad together, lived in ten different houses, shared memories of new friends and farewells, spent hours over two litters of puppies, played together, and argued together. Their interests differ from fashion modelling, books, and the body beautiful to old comics, collector's cards, and playing sports to dinosaurs, basketball, and a preoccupation with sporting detail and facts. But there has been a concentration of time spent together in a way I can never recall spending with my older siblings, allied with frequent open family discussions. All these factors will stand, I hope, as a basis for continuing friendships into their adult lives, despite periodic disjunctions.

3 Love and friendship between parents and children

Parents in traditional forms of families maintain the importance of parental distance, with father as an authoritative figure who is a disciplinarian, and mother as a nurturant figure. These parents typically love their children, but expect obedience, subordination, and deference. These children remain, in their parents' eyes, forever children, to chide about choice of partners, jobs, methods of raising children, and house design. A woman who has been through two marriages and is surviving well as a lone parent can still be greeted by her father with 'how's my little girl?'

Parents who attempt to cultivate mutual respect maintain an expectation of obedience to reasonable parental requests, but rather than being a mark of subordination, these expectations reinforce self-esteem and worth by showing children that accepting limitations on their behaviour actually develops moral character. Within a context of intimacy and affection, parents' requests for children to assist around the house, to do their required tasks and school homework, and to live within agreed household rules, take on a different flavour from the inflexible demands of the dominating disciplinarian.

Changes in parental roles are particularly pertinent to many men. Where fathers are at work and absent for much of the day, sons may create exaggerated forms of masculinity. Yet men who lovingly nurture their children show that masculinity is not compromised by overt sensitivity. Loving fathers show their children that masculinity and tenderness are not mutually exclusive, but totally compatible. Most parents, fathers included, now spend a lot of time with their children, helping with school work, talking, sharing problems, watching television, reading stories, playing games, and driving to and fro. As a result of this time spent together, there is a closer understanding of shared interests. Many parents invite their children to participate in discussions that have major implications on the family's well-being, like a relocation, a new house, household rules, duty rosters, a possible divorce, new partners, or custody questions.

These sorts of *positive family dynamics* create a milieu in which individual members become sensitive to the needs of others, giving and receiving emotional support, communicating on more than an instrumental level, so that both parents and children can learn about each other as persons, rather than just as relatives. This learning involves trusting each other to be dependable in times of need, holding each other in high regard, and providing the conditions whereby each member's individual welfare is catered for adequately. To achieve these positive dynamics, an adjustment from the 'parents know best' to an exploration of what really is in the 'child's best interests' is often required.

Where there is a mutual respect, even disputes take a different form. Rather than an attitude of parental superiority, there is more an equality of viewpoints. If parents want to develop potential friendships with their children rather than asserting a parental distance, they must be willing to listen to their children, occasionally thrusting their own view aside in order to discover who their child is, rather than what they think the child should really be. These new family dynamics require a deliberate effort to maintain the context in which the basis of loving friendships between parents and children can form, and are likely to blossom as children approach mature adulthood. Both parents and children then reap benefits of being able to share openly and freely on the basis of an affectionate regard for each other.

Commitment

The goal of developing loving friendships in families presupposes a commitment to this goal, or some sort of pledge to act on the desires which constitute the love, even when the desire is not immediately present. We all become tired and irritable at times and lose perspective. Having a pledge establishes a covenant of love, a promise of continuity that cannot be terminated just by some revelation about the object of commitment: he snores; she nags; he knows nothing about cars; she cannot cook. Legal marriage is a public declaration of this commitment to each other. Other relationships rely on personal pledges with tokens usually exchanged.

Some people see commitment as a restriction of freedom. In the playwright Henrik Ibsen's *Lady from the Sea*, there has been a long struggle between Wangel the husband, Ellida his young wife, and the Stranger, whom Ellida is fascinated with, and shares a vow. The Stranger comes to claim her. She does not want to go until her husband releases her. He tells her she can go in search of her freedom, and it is only then that she realises she can also be free with him. That is, she has always been at liberty to order her own actions; her commitment to him has not stifled her freedom.

The rejection of permanency for its own sake, 'till death do us part', is a necessary appreciation that people change, and with this change, love fades, and mutual interests dissipate. Yet sometimes, easy divorce is a cop-out—witness the megastars' marriage portfolios. We live in societies that generally do not take commitment seriously, for it is seen to tie us into tasks, jobs, groups, or other friends, not giving us the much valued individual choice. Within this framework, relationships become part of the replaceable consumer mentality: if you do not like this one, toss it out and try again.

Yet, as we noted in Chapter 5 in discussing faithfulness, the present social-sexual context raises a consciousness of the possibility of AIDS and STDs, and hence there is a caution about every new partner's sexual background. But what we are not clear about is the nature of this caution. Are these new patterns of sexual behaviour signs of a decrease in casual relationships? If so, is it based on fear of catching a sex-related illness, or fear of being caught out? Is there a genuine movement to sincere commitment?

It seems that more people are becoming aware of the limitations and shallowness of relationships based just on physical passion, desire, or lust. Clearly, just as sexual passion alone is erotic love without commitment, so too commitment alone is empty without passion or intimacy. Commitment to a partnership involves a desire to maintain a relationship, even when sexual desire might wane, but the intimate emotional bonding remains, and the partner is held in high regard. A more complete love combines *passion, intimate respect, and commitment*. This is a valid love for all good friends, where we have strong feelings for them, a deep knowledge and respect of them, and a commitment to maintaining the quality of the friendship. *Free commitment* is a powerful statement of affirmation and trust between people.

Close bonding with another individual is an expression of a central human need for intimate loving friendship. This bonding and commitment should enhance the prospect of freedom as it allows people to be themselves. Good friendships should never be so overwhelming that they constrain. With partners, the moral requirements of commitment require that faithfulness is a reasonable expectation informing the way they treat each other, that is, they do not mislead each other. Rather than restricting us, *faithfulness can be liberating*. It can broaden our freedom as in Ibsen's play, for we can trust our partners, allowing us to have close friendships with either sex, without these threatening our prime relationship.

Loving Friendship as a Basis for Social Solidarity

In conclusion, in an increasingly impersonal world where our shopkeeper, our doctor, our teacher, and our next-door neighbour frequently are as strangers to us, where we meet, recognise, wave and walk on, the family is a crucial arena for the development of a sense of *belongingness*, where meaningful companionship can develop. The choice going into the twenty-first century need not be between opposing options of individual personality and self-preference, or collective solidarity and communal interest. Rather, the problem of social solidarity, or how to support *both* individual and collective sentiment, is resolved by a collective responsibility to allowing an openness to individual difference, combined with the desire to include everyone, a particularised knowledge of interests, and a shared pursuit of interests. A commitment to the creation of good families means a commitment to the group, and to individuals in the group.

In Aristotle's language, the virtue of friendship is that which embodies a shared recognition of the pursuit of moral goals. It is this sort of sharing which is primary to community life. That is, the bonds of friendship symbolise the common project of developing social solidarity. The aim is the construction of a community of various types of families who seek the mutual growth of all their family members, a growth that sees individuals affirming themselves through collective identification, and commitment to each other. The importance of commitment extends beyond our own partners, for indeed some of us do not have a partner, to a strong motivation to maintain other meaningful relationships. Good families strive progressively toward creating *loving friendships*. Encouragement from an early age to be a loyal friend, to take commitment to others seriously, and to value those we love, provides the foundation for people who work hard to ensure that work places, social groups, and community activities are more than just places to go to, but that they are social locations where *bonds of solidarity* may develop.

10

Needing Each Other

We need each other. Interdependence is a social virtue needed to create and to sustain good families. Interdependence means there is a reliance on other family members, knowing that we need each other to ensure a healthy wellbeing. Interdependence acknowledges each family member as important, that we depend on different family members for different contributions, but that the interconnections contribute substantially to who we are, and why we need particular people in particular circumstances.

At the basis of this interdependence is the acknowledgement of a respect for others' autonomous individuality. In Chapter 3 we examined the importance of self-determination, of expressing who we are, and the freedom to determine our own behaviour and actions. In all of the chapters we have noted that when there is an emphasis on individualism, people give priority to self-interest, or to an independence seen to be free from possible constraints other relationships might impose. An individualist notion of independence does not appreciate the importance of interdependence. In this chapter I show why a *mutual respect* for others' autonomous individuality is a crucial part of moral deliberation and of *social interdependence*.

Recognising all people as worthy of respect means achieving a fine balance between appreciating one's personal *separateness from others*, and a *connectedness to others*. That is, we are quite different from those we relate to, and yet we are connected to them in important ways. The idea of respect may be a problem. If your uncle, as a prominent member of the teaching community, has been sexually molesting his pupils, or if your mother is always so drunk you can never bring your school friends home without feeling shame, or if your sister is pregnant to your brother, much of your respect for your relatives disappears. Yet, curiously, we often cannot escape the affect these relatives have on us. Because of the interdependence of family members, their situation influences us profoundly in terms of the sense of shame and hurt, the effect this has on our loss of self-confidence, or our determination to maintain personal respect, despite the odds seemingly against you.

To understand the possible benefits of mutual respect, and some of the complicated dimensions to interdependence, we explore further the relationship between our self and others in order to see how it manifests itself in families. This is important, because how we understand the self–other relationship affects either our rejection of the need for interdependence, our indifference to others, or our acceptance of the need to belong, to rely on, and to depend on others.

First, I will contrast an identity that is based on a separation from others with an identity based solely on relationships to others. This contrast has arisen in earlier chapters. In this chapter the contrast involves seeing how separateness defines itself as not really needing other people, while a relatedness can be so reliant on others that an individual's idea of self is vague.

Secondly, I will draw on this contrast to highlight how power relationships exhibit themselves in the family, often through an assertive domination over others, or a yielding subordination to others. Within these relationships the need for each other is either destructive, or not being met. These first two points highlight the fact that serious warping happens to some people within the family, and there are many reasons why people do not relate well to others, or live a life based on ethics.

Thirdly, I will show how a self-empowerment can embrace a respect for one's self and a respect for others that leads to the courage to step out of relationships that are not fruitfully interdependent, or that do not lead to the mutuality that is necessary for a healthy interdependence.

Self–Other Relationships

When we are living in a family setting, we are one of a group. Our relationships with others in the group contribute to the sort of people we are. These include relationships in the past and those in the present, satisfying relationships and destructive ones, and all the combinations between these extremes. It is how we position ourselves in these relationships, and how we view ourselves in relation to others that is our present concern. To what degree do we depend on those we live with, expecting them to rely also on us at times, or do we go our own way, expecting little from the family, and giving little in return?

Our answer to this question depends largely on how we define ourselves in relation to others. Early psychoanalytic theories of identity emphasise our emerging identity as a separation from our mother. This accentuates a separateness. Later, I show how an individuated self is more a particular way of being connected to others. As background, I trace what happens when some family members define themselves as basically separate from other family members, while others define themselves as inseparable from other family members.

1 Separation from others

When I talk of an identity based on a separation from others, I mean an identity that sees independence to be distinct from any connection to others, and considers these connections are only vaguely instrumental to personal identity. While not all men define themselves as separate from others, traditional male socialisation practices tend to encourage boys to formulate a self identity as separate from others, so that autonomy and independence is prized, and emotional connections to others are thrust aside. The message is declared that, 'big boys are tough, they don't cry, and they don't cling on to their mummy's apron strings'. Examples of this separateness were offered in Chapters 3 and 8.

Now, a self-identity that sees itself as independent and separate from others often erects a protective wall between the self and others. In not having close affiliations with others on the opposite side of the wall, this autonomous being often objectifies other people, or acts as if others are *mere objects*. In peeping over the wall, this separate being can only glimpse others, but this makes it easier to view these people in partial form, as detached beings.

This is a similar logic to what occurs in war, pornography, racism, and sexism, where the oppressor makes someone an object—the enemy, the innocent charming child, the black slave, the seductive woman. This logic enables a rationalisation of objectifying actions, precisely because of the emotional distancing involved. The person doing this becomes caught up in a tangle of personal control, not seeing the object being controlled as a person with feelings, and tears. For example, it enables someone to watch porn movies, but be angry at a daughter's nude photography session and punish her harshly. It enables a pusher to pursue those with drug habits, manipulating their dependent lifestyles, while disclaiming responsibility for their addiction.

Instead of treating other people with respect, an identity based on a separation from others does three main things.

- It splits personal autonomy from the recognition of others' autonomy. 'I know who I am, regardless of anyone else.'
- It divorces independence from moral dependence and interdependence. 'I don't need anyone else to define who I am.'
- It enables people to squash the subjectivity of another. 'I am in control of myself, and because I don't need anyone else, I can control whom I choose.'

In describing an identity based on a separation from others, I have deliberately painted an extreme picture. The consequences for those living with this sort of person are usually harsh, as they are subjected to abuse, neglect and violence—their dignity as a person is violated. In the home both men and women are likely to violate each other's respect, but in the instances of domestic violence and child sexual abuse, statistics overwhelmingly demonstrate that men are the main perpetrators, that they are more likely to view others as objects to be used at whim, whereas women are more likely to view others as subjects who need loving attention. For example, rather than thinking of a child as one's daughter, the male abuser thinks of the child merely as a sex object, or in cultures that idealise youth, he may objectify the girl as a younger version of the girl's mother. We will look at domination in more detail later. A person whose identity is based on being separated from others keeps an emotional distance from those they interact with.

2 Merging with others

You might think that people who define themselves in relationship to others, rather than in separation from others, would value interdependence, but this is not necessarily so. Whereas the traditional male stance over-emphasises self-boundaries and emotional distancing, the traditional female stance over-emphasises the relinquishing of self and emotional involvement. To continue the example used above, whereas an identity based on a separation from others builds a brick wall as a barrier, an identity based on an immersion in relationships with others lets the wall encircle them as a protective shield. The problem is whether we can see people distinctively, or whether they keep merging into the others in the circle. Protection and merging with others is often very comforting, so let me explain the possible dangers.

As outlined in Chapter 8, women often have lived much of their lives by defining themselves in terms of their capacity to care for others. They have been the protectors. For many women and men, feminine moral goodness is understood as self-sacrifice, as giving up oneself for the sake of others. So, typical socialisation patterns give girls dolls to dress, feed, and bathe, and nurses' outfits to dress up in. They thus practise service tasks, and develop strong emotional affiliations with their carers. Many women devote their entire lives to their relationships, as daughters, then as lovers, wives, and as mothers. This relational dimension is so central to this type of identity that a distinctiveness is not easily articulated.

When women are asked about themselves, many respond, 'oh, I'm just a housewife', or 'I'm only Peter's wife', or 'I'm simply Fiona's mother'. Caring for others is good, but it should not have to be at the expense of developing one's self. Women often see their moral worth only in terms of their caring for others. This may blind women to the types of relationships they are in, that their identity may be defined by relations which are harmful, exploitative, or destructive. Rather than an interdependence of autonomous beings, caring for the dependent can lead to an identity that is extremely dependent on relationships to others.

To summarise, to see the self–other relationship as distinct from one's identity leads to the independent separation from others, where we do not think we really need others in any important sense. Yet to see the self–other relationship as totally contingent on other relationships leads to a merging of self in one's nexus of relationship, without proper regard to how these relationships affect the autonomous self. Neither option leads to an appreciation of interdependence, where we all acknowledge our need for each other. Indeed, the extremes of these positions lead to domination and to subordination.

Domination, Subordination, and Power

Domination and subordination occur in different ways in different families. Domination controls, it wields power over others, and it constrains individuality. We become too scared to be ourselves. Subordination means a lack of the opportunity to be self-directive, and to take personal responsibility for the conditions of one's actions, so the subordinate yields to the person who is controlling.

Domestic violence

Domestic violence is a vivid example where domination and control exist alongside submission and dependency. The term domestic violence can include psychological, economic, social physical, and sexual abuse. While both women and men can engage in psychological and social abuse, and physically abuse young children, it is primarily men as chief breadwinners who economically abuse women, and who perpetuate the criminally offensive physical and sexual violence in families. Examples of these abuses follow:

Psychological abuse:	– you're an ugly, fat bitch – you're a hopeless mother/father/child – I'll kill the kids if you leave me
Economic abuse:	– inadequate money to pay basic household bills – making a partner account for every bit of money spent – giving the non-earner no money, but doing the shopping together, and then paying
Social abuse:	– refusing to give a house key – humiliating a family member in public – ignoring a relative in social gatherings
Physical abuse:	– broken bones – bruises (disguised as accidents) – scratches, cuts, burns – deliberate starvation
Sexual abuse:	– sexual harassment and assault – forced oral, vaginal, anal sex – rape within marriage.

While all these forms of abuse have devastating consequences on their victims, the emotional and social costs of physical and sexual abuse are particularly great. They are major causes of marital and familial breakdown. For women who are forced to leave violent contexts, dependence on emergency welfare, housing, and income support services almost always spells,[1] if not poverty, at least a substantial drop in their standard of living.

Those women who stay in violent family contexts do so for various reasons. They often fear that their children will suffer emotionally and financially through not having a father. These men may appear gentle and kind to the women in public, and are sometimes considerate to their children, hence often these women hide their pain as a secret, even from their children. There is frequently a strong emotional attachment toward the violent man, and a desperate hope that the partner will change. They often still love him, despite his violence. Many women fear correctly that they will be subject to retaliatory abuse if they leave. Some women feel somehow as if they are to blame, or find it hard to share their suffering with other family members, for fear they will not be believed. Lack of knowledge of legal rights and alternatives, and lack of financial resources, also leaves many women with no option other than to remain in violent family circumstances.

If the family is supposed to be a haven from the harsh outside world, a place of love, of security, of warmth and of belonging, why does violence prevail in so many families? One answer to this is that in mythology, and in reality, masculinity is still associated with domination, and sexual dominance with personal success. Male stereotypical characteristics like strength, toughness, aggression, forcefulness, and dominance permeate western and many other cultures. Prime signifiers of traditional masculinity, like work, sport, alcohol, power over women, and sexual conquest, all involve if not violent tendencies, certainly aggressive ones. In a material culture of domination, where we accept the existence of male mastery and brutality on our television and cinema screens, the reasons why we accept so much violence often escape us.

Power and consent

Jessica Benjamin, a feminist theorist, explains how *domination* is a two-way process, a system involving the participation of *those who submit* to power, as well as *those who exercise* it. In the traditional family form, this system cultivates the autonomous authority of the man as head and as boss, where he expects deference and often lashes out when it is not forthcoming. This is a notion of independent masculine selfhood that is indifferent to inequalities of power and situation. Within these gendered power relations, the dependency of women and children are cultivated, creating a climate where they are vulnerable to abuse. The liberal ideal of non-interference of the state into domestic lives, and the high value placed on privacy, has hidden the extent of this abuse, an issue welfare policy and legal procedures are starting to confront.

Domination refuses to accept the personhood of the other. Yet submission does not necessarily imply consent. Consent is an active, willing agreement. Submission often is based not on consent, but on fear, such as in controversial date-rape situations, where a 'no' is interpreted as a seductive 'yes'. Compliance may involve knowingly giving in, fully aware of the consequences of not submitting. This is not a passive yielding. Others may submit more actively to any number of possible activities, thinking it is expected of them, or wanting to escape the responsibilities of decision-making. Not all domination is physically violent. As listed above, psychological, economic and social abuse prevails, suppressing the dignity of others. The cycle of family domination and abuse must be halted. There is *no place for violence in the family*. No one has the right to own or to sexually possess another, no right to violate or to control another. To halt this cycle of domination and subordination, we need to break down patterns of power.

Power relations

The family is a site for power, whereby people try to change, influence, or direct what happens to others. Not all power is harmful. Parents wield a lot of power and influence in the basic socialisation of children, directing them to things they should learn, try, or know. When used with practical wisdom, this sort of power is for the good of others. The reasons why family members strive for powerful control over others are varied. As noted, there are strict gender stereotypes that affect notions of power, like the social expectations for men to let women know who is master. Men with deep psychological insecurities may compensate by being dictatorial. Power is often attributed to the breadwinner. In dual income families, men are consistently the chief earners. As women's earning capacity increases, so does her power in decision-making.

Gender stereotypes for women foster passivity, submissiveness, and dependence, reinforcing unequal power relations between men and women. Children too can often be very powerful, manipulating their parents' emotions, playing off one parent against the other, dividing families by their determination to get their own way, an issue with difficult practical ramifications both in families where the parents are together or have separated. Our families of origin often wield an uncanny power, playing on guilt, social expectations, and cultural norms. This may be particularly pertinent in cross-cultural partnerships.

People use various tactics to control others, and to get others to do what they want. Coercive power often forces people to do things against their wishes. Parents frequently do not give their children an option. There may be a threat of physical punishment or some privilege withdrawn for not doing as they are told. Physical threats can be very frightening, particularly when the threat has been carried out before. A remote-control gadget hurled in frustration at the wall has a different effect from a plate deliberately thrown at someone's face. Angry outbursts and violent tempers can be very powerful means to get others to concede to individual wishes. So too can the silent treatment, where someone refuses to talk, or even to acknowledge another. This muteness may persist for days, weeks, months, until a rigid pattern emerges that seems almost unbreakable.

Constant criticism of others, putting them down or humiliating them can act as a control. Scapegoating, blaming others, can also be a form of manipulation. Being helplessly dependent when one could be otherwise evokes sympathy from others who rush to help out. The more limited one's alternatives, the less power people have in relationships. Children regularly are very powerless. Some children wield power by manipulating their parents' kindness, or by their refusal to comply with known expectations. An economically powerful husband may insist that his wife does not pursue the career she trained for. A bachelor who has never left home may feel under the sway of his controlling parents who are dependent on his care. A woman with dependent children and no access to independent income may feel totally helpless in the face of a dominating, powerful partner.

Even the idea of a balance of power which is acceptable in a family context is problematic. It does not take into account the likelihood of accepting an imbalance. John Scanzoni, a sociologist, gives a useful definition of 'partner equality': 'equity *satisfaction* with the perceived *justice* of the situation'. You can imagine a household that has verbally agreed to divide chores equally but, in practice, one person starts to realise their tasks are more time-consuming, energy-consuming, or financially inequitable, so dissatisfaction mounts. Partner equality is reached only when there is agreement and satisfaction that the arrangements are fair. When equity is the ultimate goal, there must be frequent communication, negotiation, co-operation, and flexibility, and the realisation that compromises and concessions are inevitable. This is time-consuming, arduous and fraught with conflict. Nevertheless, 'everything should be negotiable, except the idea that everything is negotiable'. In this open context, there is no place for relationships of domination and subordination, power and powerlessness.

Mutual Recognition and Empowerment

Power plays obstruct interdependence so that families do not fully appreciate the extent to which *we need each* other. A positive view of relationships, and of the interaction between one's self and others must exist for interdependence within the family to be a realistic goal. This is not possible in relationships where one attempts to suppress, dominate, control, or subdue the other. A household might be frustrated in achieving interdependence by one disruptive or destructive person.

What we need is a revised notion of self-autonomy, or the freedom to define who we are, and to shape our own lives, one that emerges in the social contexts in which we find ourselves. It is not just that we continually encounter others in our daily lives, but that the others we relate with help to shape who we are and what we do. This is equally valid for good relationships as it is for poor relationships. We are simultaneously separate individuals and we are intrinsically connected to others. Take away the separateness and we have an identity blurred into others. Take away the connections, and we have a lone, dominating, or isolated individual.

Reciprocity

We all yearn for recognition—to be known ourselves, and to be recognised for who we are, and we long to know others in their unique distinctiveness. A *mutual recognition* between people acknowledges a sense of self as being differentiated from others despite being intrinsically related to others. For example, a man has a unique personality that being a husband, a father, or a manager only partly reflects. A woman is not just a daughter, a wife, or a mother, she is a person in her own right, and being a daughter, a wife, and a mother influences the sort of person she is. A firm sense of self is crucial, for without it there is a submission to others, or an attempt to assert the self through the control of others. Both are a sign of weakness, the giving in, and the domination of others. Without a clear sense of self, we cannot assess the relationships we are in, especially those which are abusive or oppressive, and where we need to withdraw.

As the philosopher Claudia Card reminds us, there are extensive examples of intimate partner abuse and exploitative intimate peer relationships, 'where one accepts but fails to reciprocate another's caring, without the excuses of infancy, very old age, or disability'. She defines the goal of reciprocity as 'doing to or for another, something that is either equivalent in value or the same thing that the other did to or for oneself'. Reciprocity in political theorist Carol Gould's terms can be used as a model of non-exploitative social relations. Reciprocity does not just explain what goes on in caring relationships, it acts as a standard that allows us to criticise relationships of domination or submission, power or powerlessness as defective forms of social interaction. This is not a reciprocity that is instrumental, that says, 'I'll scratch your back, if you scratch mine'. Rather, *mutuality* is the developed form of reciprocity where relationships are seen as important ends in themselves, *affirming our need for each other,* proving it by practical examples in practical contexts.

Mutual recognition thus entails a dynamic notion of each person's independence. Being able to act on our own volition does not imply that we have no need for others. Rather, an *individuated sense of self* is a particular way of *being connected to others*. With these connections we can take pleasure in the differences between one person and another, the differences between men and women, between men and men, between women and women, between different children, and between different classes, cultures, races, and family members. Appreciating differences can introduce a source of deep enrichment, an appreciation of the endless variety of human relationships. Mutual recognition also enables us to relate as equals, or in the case of parent and young child relations, we can relate as people of equal moral worth. Mutual recognition acknowledges each family member for who they are, who in turn, acknowledge each other family member similarly.

Self-empowerment

Where there is a *mutual recognition of others*, there is an *empowerment of interdependent beings that bonds people together.* Empowered people have an autonomy that repudiates separateness, control or domination; they refuse to be manipulated, coerced, or exploited. Self-empowerment emerges from understanding our connections to those about us. Indeed it sees personal strength to be facilitated through interaction with others. This is not a power over others, but a *personal inner strength* and this self-empowerment can occur even where there is not mutual recognition. This inner strength is the basis from which those who experience daily harassment, abuse, and destructive victimisation can take control of the situation, rather than merely respond to each situation. This also is the basis from which those who are privileged to be living in a situation of mutual recognition enjoy varying expressions of difference and feed off each other's moral character.

Good families create contexts in which self-empowerment can occur. Just as domination and submission do not foster interdependence, so powerlessness also is destructive of personal empowerment. To realise our inner strength, we need to feel comfortable with those around us. When we feel awkward, threatened, or embarrassed, we do not act freely. What enables us to be empowered is positive relationships with others, not isolation from others. That is, dependence is a precondition of autonomy; it prevents the development of the separate individualist I have criticised; it confirms our vulnerability as an expression of humanity. Just as babies are dependent on adults for physical sustenance, so too adults are dependent on others for emotional and spiritual growth. Our empowerment develops in the context of relations with others who nurture this capacity, and who depend on our nurture. *Dialogue* is a crucial component in this context, discussing, explaining, bargaining, negotiating, compromising, and being prepared to withhold personal power in order to reach an agreement.

Interdependence

We are individuals who are intrinsically tied to other social beings. The idea and practices of interdependence stand as a basis of creative interaction for good families and for good social bonds. How can we achieve this goal? It involves men redefining their masculinity in ways that do not depend on an autonomous identity as a separation from others, or a domination over others, but in ways that acknowledge the need for negotiation, co-operation, and a sensitivity to others' situations. This requires active parenting by men who are fathers, from childbirth on, to facilitate mutual attachments, and to prevent them ever wanting to hurt a vulnerable being. Men who are not fathers play an important part in interdependent networks, in being caring brothers, uncles, lovers, and friends.

Likewise women must claim their subjectivity. They must stop defining their identity solely through relational means as daughter, wife, and/or mother, while acknowledging that these roles are important in influencing their identity. When women come to expect relations of equality, they will be reluctant to tolerate relations of abuse. Children must be encouraged to move from a dependency to an independence that nurtures the context for interdependency. This is a movement from being totally reliant on others to being reliant on one's self, to being *mutually reliant on connections of importance.*

The vision of mutual recognition of equal subjects, of realising our interdependence, is a logic of paradox. Our need to affirm our separateness from others requires a social context of dependence on others. We realise ourselves as individuals only through being intrinsically tied to others. We are who we are through our relations with others in specific contexts. I realise myself as daughter, sister, wife, mother, aunt, niece, and friend through my specific relationships. There is no individuality except through our relationships, and relationships shape our unique identity.

This idea of *intrinsic connectedness* seems to be more acceptable on a global scale; for example, an ecological disaster in a major ocean has repercussions on ecosystems world-wide. A horrifying civil war leaves its people as penniless, homeless refugees, with neighbouring nations wavering about their obligations to these people. Most of us see famine and the devastation caused by natural disasters as global concerns. We marvel at satellite technological advances that entertain us and assist in scientific and medical research. We watch a major sports event, or even a school sports day and admire the co-ordination of players, coaches, referees, canteen workers, and the crowd itself.

Yet sometimes we can stand back and distance ourselves from these global issues. In our own communities we despair of the fragmentation, the competing needs, and the fleeting meeting of strangers. We need to embrace an ideal of interdependence as a basis for public concerns like economic considerations, trade, export, and political relations, and as an ideal for community relationships, and for domestic concerns, social bonds, and familial relationships. The only way to come closer to realising the ideal is to start practising it.

For example, to work out the concrete needs of people in our communities we need to know what distinguishes us all, how our needs are affected by our gender, race, class, generation, cultural differentials, personal preferences, and economic situation. The more we know about each other, the more viable will be the outcome of our deliberations. The attempt to make intricate connections can also confuse us, as extreme differences become conspicuous. Anyway, the contact is an important part of social interdependence. The contact can lead to an ethic of solidarity that appreciates differences and similarities, and our mutual need for each other.

Interdependence confirms simultaneously our:
- autonomy and sense of attachment
- our independence and our connections
- our individuality and our social bonds.

It is in good families where this interdependence is initially learnt. When children are exposed to parents who practise an *autonomous connectedness* in both the public and private spheres, where they have claimed a self-empowerment that does not need to dominate, suppress, repress, or squash others, and where all family members are respected for who they are, then the context is created for loving nurturance within an interdependent network.

11

Having and Owing

In this and the concluding chapter, two of the major recurring themes in this book come together, namely the relationship between the individual and the broader social networks, and the tendency of individualism to undermine this relationship. What we have noted in earlier chapters is that a person's unique individuality is more likely to flourish when the person is exposed to a variety of warm, positive social situations. We are *social individuals* who express our selves in relation to those who differ from us. A strong sense of self provides the basis from which we see the needs of others and respond morally. Connections and responses to others are an integral dimension of our sense of self-identity. When we lose sight of the importance of these connections, and concentrate only on our selves, the social basis of morality is undermined. Instead, we get a world of competing individuals, often ruthlessly shoving each other away in order to be the one standing on top. In order to prevent selfish self-assertion, we need to balance *individual rights* with *social responsibilities*.

Individual Rights

The protection of individuals' rights is important. The United Nations Universal Declaration of Human Rights is the 'recognition of the inherent dignity and of the equal and inalienable rights of all members of the human family', and it stands as the foundation of freedom, justice, and peace in the world. Human rights are normative, that is, they provide a moral model for the way in which we as individuals or as groups are to be regarded with dignity and treated with respect. They are based on a minimal ethical code as outlined in Chapter 1. In discussing this code, we noted that basic human rights are necessary to realise a range of human ends, like the need for shelter, nutrition, health, warmth, clothing, education, spirituality, and creativity. Societies ought to accept the obligation to ensure that these basic needs are provided when families themselves cannot provide them. As Virginia Held, political theorist, expresses it, 'rights do concern the basic minimums to which every citizen is entitled and below which none should ever have to fall'. Rights are not necessarily egoistic. They require that each person act with due regard for others' rights and that the provision of basic rights is part of social co-operation.

Why then do we hear a lot about the United Nations Article 1, that 'all human beings are born free and equal in dignity and rights', but not so much about Article 29.1, that 'everyone has duties to the community in which alone the free and full development of personality is possible'? The cry for rights is vocal—child rights, gay rights, father rights, custody rights, disabled persons' rights. These are important rights, but what often happens is that the cry for these rights becomes single focused, self-assertive, and blind to the often conflicting needs of others. Claims for child rights may clash with adult rights and sibling rights; father rights and custody rights may clash with mother rights and children's rights; and the list goes on. The cry for individual rights has become out of control, in that it frequently is divorced from the mutual respect of other rights, and the corresponding duties that attach to rights. Accordingly, it is interpreted as the right to choose, or the right to choose whatever I prefer, or the right to do as I please. The rhetoric and practice of this belief is conspicuous in many of our young people.

1 Children's rights

In older family patterns where there were large numbers of children born, and where children were an integral part of the household economy, the focus was necessarily on the physical survival of the family unit. This often remains the pattern in poorer rural areas and in 'developing' societies. In western families, children generally are part of a calculated plan. The emphasis is on developing the individuality of children. From the time the baby is born, individualised one-to-one attention usually is lavished on the baby, and much time, energy and money is expended on creating stimulating conditions for early growth. This is good.

But what often happens is that from the time the child is starting to make self-assertive claims, the parents are bemused by the cute confidence of this 'grown-up child' who knows exactly how to get his/her own way. For busy, tired parents, it is often easier to give into a child's demands than to stop and explain why they cannot do something. Parents of an only child, or of a young child with a much older sibling, are often stunned to see their child at a nursery school or day care, or at a friend's place, hitting, punching, or kicking another child in fierce refusal to share. Unwittingly, parents are compliant in this possessiveness. Our grandparents may have been content with a ball, a book, some crayons, some marbles, a skipping rope, and a soft cuddly toy, but witness the toys many of our children have. Our children are part of the 'give me more, I want it now' generations, and rights become meshed with this materialistic mentality. Economists, retailers, and the media send messages that a high rate of consumption is crucial for a sound economy.

Instead of children being 'seen but not heard', a repressive dictum, the wilful tantrum throwing, the sheer defiance, and the refusal to obey is the norm in many households. While parents retain some degree of authority over their children, where there is still some discipline and restraint over the often unreasonable pursuit of self-interest, the total abuse of individual rights is kept in check. But one of the myths of modernity is that of the possibility of absolute freedom. Our young people, caught in the twilight of childhood and adulthood, crave freedom, which many define as the absence of constraint. In its pursuit they cling on to self-assertive individual rights, basically as the freedom to do and to say as they please. Teenagers who define freedom this way abusively defy any attempt to curb language, behaviour, drug usage, clothing style, leisure pursuits, study habits, acquaintances, curfew times, and ways of relating to others.

One of the chief problems with this orientation is that freedom only makes sense within *boundaries*, and this is hard to explain to children. In sport you have freedom to explore the position you play within the rules of the game. As a car driver, you are free to drive within the limits of road regulations. Minors, with only a vague understanding of the boundaries between rights and responsibilities, freedom and selfish individualism, often become slaves to individual desire. Parents can ground them, but they often escape out of a bedroom window. Parents might deprive them of their allowance (often assumed by children as their right), but they can shop-lift, borrow, or get others who have money to buy them what they want. If parents try to punish them, they often squeal 'that's not fair', which being translated means 'I'm not getting my own way'. Rather than being free to pursue life's options, they become slaves to the ruthless pursuit of self-interest. Individual rights are prized as paramount.

The state plays a conflicting role in this assertion of rights. On the one hand, it claims that parents are responsible for children in a legal and moral sense until they are eighteen. Yet it does not always support reasonable parental authority, and young adults exploit loopholes in the welfare system, and ambiguities in the juvenile justice system. On the other hand, educational policies emphasising children's rights teach children they have a right to refuse compliance with behaviour with which they are not comfortable. Not all children come from a position of privilege where the principles of good families are second nature. Even children from privileged families may reject ethical codes. For some children, education may be their only access to discussions on self-worth, dignity, and their right to refuse certain behaviour, not only inappropriate sexual behaviour, but unreasonable, non-negotiable requests from their parents.

I am concerned that education programmes often forget the equal importance of responsibilities, or children strive not to hear, and rights translates too quickly into a refusal to accept any legitimate discipline or restriction of personal desires. When this happens, parents are frequently powerless to discipline their children. It is not that they are complacent; often their children just refuse to respect parents' right to define moral boundaries. Yet if children overstep society's boundaries it is the parents who are deemed to be at fault. Society often resorts particularly to mother blaming.

Yes, children have rights, all the basic rights, particularly of protection, provision, and affirmation of self-respect. But *with rights come responsibilities*, and being accountable for personal actions as well as not suppressing the rights of others, like the rights of siblings and parents. An excessive emphasis on self-assertive individual rights, without an accompanying sense of responsibility to others, misses much of what we are as moral agents, that we grow into moral maturity. With this growth comes the realisation that morality concerns the way we relate to others, and thus the acceptance of the consequences of our treatment of others.

2 Privacy rights

Some of the reasons why individual rights dominate not only youth, but adults as well, is the liberal democratic priority given to the individual, to freedom, and to personal choice. These are important dimensions to our life as citizens of a democratic polity. So what goes wrong? The liberal right to choose is inadequate as the sole driving force of a society. It gives no guidance as to how people should make their choices, or what might be a good or a bad choice. In the name of toleration and of democratic pluralism, the state adopts a neutrality about the good. It recognises our privacy rights, the rights inherent in personhood that respect our self-autonomy, and ensure minimal state intervention.

In a positive sense, privacy rights affirm the importance of uncoerced decision-making. The collapse of communism has testified to the value of individual choice and the integrity of citizen life. We do not like the state dictating to us; we like to make our own choices. But, in a negative sense, privacy rights reinforce two significant problems for our project of devising strategies for creating good families. First, the 'right to be left alone' fosters an individualistic culture of isolated individuals. Secondly, the moral good is privatised. Let me expand on these two consequences.

First, the right to be left alone basically says, 'I am who I am to do as I please, leave me alone, I am going to do as I want'. This liberal ideal of non-intervention unintentionally reinforces actual family inequalities. Historically, privacy rights were seen to accrue to male heads of households to regulate their families as they thought fit. A man's family was considered to be part of his property. As women acquire citizenship rights of the vote, property ownership, and an independent income, this cult of privacy affects them also, and many women choose to live as if they are isolated individuals.

Our society places a high value on individual freedom, self-determination, and the right to choose, and the family is considered a highly autonomous unit. Any encroachment on this autonomy is seen as an erosion of this basic value, an assault on the social institution of the family. No one has absolute freedom to choose and, in a society of individuals, conflicting rights are inevitable. Yet, the state's exercise of its protective function towards victims of abuse can come about only through interference with the family's autonomy. It has taken a long time for the police force to begin to break down its resistance to intervening in violent 'domestic' disputes. State intervention into the family is still seen by many people as a territorial invasion.

To overstate the picture, what we have in the west are masses of private individuals, living in small households, often in large houses in suburban settings. As Bill Jordan, political theorist, puts it, 'their moral horizons stretch little further than their garden fence; they are concerned about each other, and wish their neighbours well, though not well enough to seek their well-being in any active way'. Many of us hardly know the names of people living near us. Even many of our social associations with others as pleasure pursuits are supplied by market forces. We go to the movies, sports matches, nightclubs, restaurants, or on shopping excursions, where we are surrounded by people, but with whom we have no meaningful contact, a mere community of strangers, and we retreat back to the privacy of our personal space. In valuing our privacy, we are left alone, *a culture of isolated individuals.*

Secondly, in this culture, *the moral good is privatised*; it is left entirely in the hands of individuals, or separate family groups to decide what they see to be good family practices. Freedom of choice and self-preference are the chief moral arbiters. This is a major mark of social change. In traditional societies, social and moral rules still are clearly defined by religion, custom, or ritual. In complex industrial societies, where widespread adherence to religion, cultural convention, and ceremony has diminished, we face an agony of choice, and a confusion as to *how* we should decide on important issues. When moral education is left to private choice, the generalisable lessons once accepted by most people diminish, and there are fewer guidelines for organising social rules. A major consequence of this privatisation of morality is that there is no way of deciding between competing rights' claims, like foetal rights versus mother rights, parental rights to discipline versus children's rights to experiment, or a single father's right to employment versus his children's right to quality care.

When ideas of the good and how we should decide on appropriate ways of deliberating between competing claims to rights are left to isolated individuals, the moral content of our reflections is reduced to mere self-preference. This is not to say that sometimes what we prefer is not appropriate, right, or good. But often it might be morally impoverished and without meaningful social content. Sometimes we might make decisions that our society would not condone as moral. It is through our joint action and ways of knowing that we create our morality.

I agree with Elizabeth Fox Genovese in her critique of individualism when she says, 'it could be argued that the free play of individual right may well have acted as the single most powerful solvent of moral consensus'. As she argues further, it is only by grounding the idea of personal liberty in the collectivity, in recognising that there cannot be individual freedom (only licence) without community discipline, that we can 'hope to enact laws that recognise liberties as interdependent and as inseparable from social responsibilities'. The privacy rights of isolated individuals do not create *moral frameworks for responsible societies*. Individual rights and social responsibilities must be conjoined.

Social Responsibilities

To understand the combination of individual rights and social responsibilities, good families understand the importance of having and owing, that there are ties, balances, and checks that need to be made between:

- individual rights and social responsibilities
- individuality and sociality
- individual differences and commonalities
- personal preferences, interests, and desires, and family, group, and community needs
- self-interest and social duty.

Both sides of these contrasts are important to living a moral life, and should be incorporated into practical judgements in family life. The first side takes into account the individual rights and preferences, the fulfilment of which so often competes or conflicts with other persons' rights and preferences. One person in a family likes the music up loud; another gets irritable with this. One person has favourite television programmes; another person wants another channel. One partner is an early riser and an early sleeper; the other person likes to party late. Some family members like the rural peace and quiet; others like the hustle and bustle of city life. Appreciating an ethic of rights is to balance competing claims of one's self with those of others we live and mix with, looking for ways whereby we can incorporate individual desires as much as possible without hurting one another.

This is possible only when an *ethic of rights* exists alongside an *ethic of responsibilities*. The second side of the above contrasts takes into account the social responsibilities we owe to others, that in a family context, different demands and needs have to be taken into account. This realisation of the importance of responsibilities to others sees that our individuality connects with our social life, that our connections to others are an intrinsic part of who we are. An ethic of responsibilities also rests on many of the issues discussed in earlier chapters, like the problem of inclusion, of minimising hurt, and of being compassionate and affectionately caring.

In family settings, as in other social contexts, it is not easy to include those of very different ages, and those with different likes and dislikes. In families we spread our favours, time, money, energy, and concerns among many. We often avoid being concerned with others if it is at the expense of our own interests. Alternatively, some people can be preoccupied by the interests of others, ignoring their own needs. As noted in other chapters, this is a mistake many women have made in devoting themselves to their husbands, their children, and their grandchildren at the expense of any independent pursuit of other personal interests. This self-sacrifice is not the social responsibility I am referring to, that tries to balance:

- individual rights with social responsibilities—what we have as individuals, and what we owe to others
- our individuality with our sociability—how we express our distinctive separateness and our affable relationships with others
- individual differences with what we share in common—how we differ from others, and how we are similar to others
- personal desires with the needs of others—what we want ourselves, and what others require
- self-interest with social duty—thinking just of ourselves, and thinking of the tasks we are actually bound to do for others.

When we combine this mixture so that it becomes a habitual part of our moral character, there is a real attempt to take into account *both* individual interests and the group's interests. This is complicated. It is so much easier just to look after one's self. But a fine balance between individual rights and social responsibilities is made vivid in accepting that we owe particular people particular obligations.

Moral Obligations

For many people 'obligation' is a dirty word. It runs right across the grain of their search for individual fulfilment, individual choice, and the chance to do as they please. It implies having to do things out of duty, as a burden, something that constrains free play, or a requirement that stultifies free choice. I want to rescue the idea of obligation from these negative connotations, and show how it is a positive concept, crucial for the social co-operation of society. The stronger our attachments to people, the stronger our sense of obligation. Indeed, it is our sense of connectedness to others that provides us with a sense of common purpose that sustains the basis for mutual obligation.

Michael Sandel, political theorist, draws an important qualification. He says there are 'natural duties' we owe to all humans, such as to alleviate suffering, pain, and hardship where possible. This duty is irrespective of our relationship to the stranger, the passer-by, casual acquaintances, or those in the developing nations. If we are at the beach and we see a person drowning, we have a natural duty to assist whether by throwing a rope, a life buoy, diving in to help, or calling the life-saver. If we hear of natural disasters of flood, earthquake, landslide, fire, or drought, and it is in our capacity to assist physically, or through donation, we ought to help.

The basis of this natural duty is the respect we have for fellow humans, the respect that is the foundation of the minimal ethical code I have repeatedly referred to. This is a mutual respect. We do not assist just so the person suffering might assist us when we need it, but we do assist knowing that mutual respect for human dignity is the basis of these duties. It is an injunction to recognise common human vulnerabilities, that fortune and fate is morally arbitrary; no one deserves sickness, accidents, trauma, or premature death. Natural duty is a form of compassion that acknowledges that one's own possibilities in life are similar to those of the person suffering.

Our duties within families to people we know well differ from those minimal duties that we owe to all. Within families there are three major strengths of obligations.

- Weak obligations exist in a family that has not even respected basic natural duties.

- Medium-level obligations exist in groups that consider the family to be important, whatever the particular relationships are like.

- Strong obligations emerge from strong allegiances to particular persons.

When we are talking about obligations, we are exploring three questions.

- How can I care adequately for all those family members I somehow feel responsible for?
- Who should I feel responsible for?
- What is the nature of this responsibility?

Let us explore the differences between weak, medium, and strong obligations in the light of these questions, remembering that there are intermediate categories between these levels.

Before discussing weak obligations, I need to qualify the nature of family obligations. This qualification is relevant particularly to readers who have unhappy family memories. Close associations over long periods of time form unique relationships which are not always healthy. Many children spend a lifetime trying to escape the oppression, repression, abuse, stultification, violence, inhibitions, neglect, indifference, psychological manipulation, and verbal humiliation of their upbringing. Some adults spend a lifetime trying to cope with the misery and emotional hurt inflicted on them by an ex-partner. Some parents spend a lifetime trying to work out why their child became a drug addict, a prostitute, a criminal, a hard, bitter person, or committed suicide. I have argued consistently that morality must take into account social context, and one's background is an important part of this context. Even strict dictums like 'do not murder' adapt to context, and thus permit the killing of another in self-defence, or to protect the life of another.

So the moral guidelines that we should take seriously in our family obligations need to consider each family member's unique historical context. The father who has been irresponsible in his parenting, and has sexually abused his daughter, has forfeited the right to expect her to feel family obligations to him, despite the fact that this family might actively demand that she should forgive. What about the mother who has criticised her son daily, never giving him one encouraging word? What does this son owe his mother? And what of the respected businessman, active in community politics and church leadership, always polite and sweet to his wife in public, but who ridicules her constantly at home? His wife fears his approaching retirement. What does this wife really owe her husband?

Weak obligations

In this first category of *weak* obligations, there seem to be three levels of responses in families that have not even respected all basic natural duties. First, the *minimal requirements of natural duties* that we owe other humans simply by virtue of possessing dignity of personhood remains, and this we owe to all regardless of our relationship to the person. So this means that we should not leave an accident victim trapped, a lost child wandering around, or a beggar unfed. Similarly, despite the abuse we may have been subjected to, we should assist our relatives in ensuring that the minimal requirements of basic needs are met. This may be painfully difficult to accept. Many people cope by avoidance. Others, knowing that basic needs have been met, understandably minimise or eliminate all personal contact, perhaps writing an occasional letter or birthday card. When family members are not willing to meet basic needs, outsiders, either private or religious charities, government provisions, or international organisations have to meet the differences.

Secondly, and this too is difficult, family members should be prepared to *change their feelings and responses* if the particular family member apologises, repents, and changes behaviour. This might happen for all sorts of reasons—growing up, realising the stupidity of one's mistakes, the passing of time, reflection on one's past, loneliness, or new relationships that implore one to make amends. Forgiving, particularly after a lifetime of being abused, rejected, or neglected, is formidable but, as we have seen in earlier chapters, forgiving is an important family virtue, although understandably there will be certain actions that appear to defy the possibility of forgiveness. The attitude of young prostitutes in Asian countries who are sold by their families for much needed income is an interesting example. Despite hating their job, they usually return to their families on holiday laden with appropriate gifts, realising that their families' livelihood often depends on their sordid work.

The third response to weak obligation often occurs as old age or severe illness approaches, and either the abuser or the abused is desperate to *make peace before it is too late* and one only has a conscience to live with. Our conscience can nag us, reminding us of the rightness or of the mistake of a particular action. Not knowing how to initiate the peace-making process after decades of silence or animosity often frustrates the endeavour, and a brother commits suicide, a father has a heart attack, a mother refuses contact, a daughter overdoses, and it is too late. To summarise, where family members have not even respected basic natural duties, weak obligations suffice.

Medium-level obligations

A second *medium* type of obligation comes with a commitment to the broad notion of family. This is evident particularly in certain cultures where simply because you share a local village, or a family name, either through blood kin or marriage, this binds you as a group. When there is a celebration, a wedding, a birthday party, or a christening you are expected to be there, no matter how well you know the celebrants. It also means that when someone needs help—a job, financial assistance, a place to stay, or protection, there is an obligation to assist for no other reason than that '*you are family*'. The strengths of these bonds that bind people together are indisputable, and can be a rich source of delight, but they have not always been used for good motives. They have often been the basis of illegal protection rackets, and of inter-familial antagonism between rival entrepreneurs. Perhaps another example of this medium level of obligation comes with the idea of obligations to support one's children, which do not end with separation or divorce. A parent remains part of a child's family story so that, even when separated, obligations remain.

Strong obligations

The third type of obligation is a *strong* one. It is based on *allegiances to particular persons* that result in types of obligations that exceed the mere natural duties we owe to all humans. Our attachment to significant others, and to those familial relationships we are committed to, contributes to the persons we are. Close associations over long periods of time form unique relationships. Admittedly these are not always healthy, but we have dealt with these. Here, I want to talk about good family relationships, for these are expressive of a good which is unique to those special relationships. As Lawrence Blum, author on the emotions and relationships, reminds us, the moral dimensions of these relationships, or how we choose to act with regard to the good, is inevitably bound with the particular qualities of the relationship.

Assuming good relationships, think of the different demands, special responsibilities and moral obligations of:

- a partner towards their partner
- an older sibling towards a younger sibling
- a father towards his child
- a mother towards her child
- a child towards a parent
- a grandparent towards a grandchild
- an uncle or an aunt towards a nephew or a niece
- a cousin towards a cousin
- a step-parent towards a step-child
- a social parent towards an adopted or a foster child.

Each of these relationships is quite different. With the weak and medium versions, obligation was something one had to do; it was a form of duty, there was no choice. In this strong sense of obligation, familial responsibilities are freely chosen as a sign of one's commitment to special relationships. That is, because of one's strong ties to particular family members, and the realisation that there are many things we ought to do for each other, we freely choose to do them.

For example, a partner, in affirming a commitment to another partner, is obliged to show signs of this commitment through the sorts of virtues we have discussed by:

- allowing a freedom of self-expression
- including the other, being flexible, and willing to negotiate
- being faithful, loyal, and reliable
- being truthful, honest, and trustworthy
- being forgiving, just, and merciful
- showing affectionate care, and intimacy
- being loving, and being a good friend
- valuing their interdependence
- respecting mutual rights, and taking seriously their responsibilities to the other.

While I say that a committed partner is obliged to be virtuous in this manner, I am suggesting that because of the strong attachment to the other, the partner freely undertakes this obligation. While an obligation always implies a sense of what one *must do*, the partner could not consider doing otherwise. This is something they have to do, but they *freely choose to do* so. When these obligations are mutual, willingly accepted by both partners, a firm foundation is established for a loving, moral partnership.

To expand this example of freely chosen obligation, there is a unique aspect of familial mutuality that extends beyond the natural duties we owe to all. Claudia Mills, writer on values and public policies, talks of a 'cycle of familial reciprocity'. She is addressing what it is humanly decent to do, particularly in the light of an ageing population where we live healthier and longer. She maintains that 'the explanation of why children might owe care to their ageing parents may lie in some notion of what families fundamentally are all about'; that is, they are co-operative arrangements with a set of goods of mutual benefit to family members. Legitimate expectations thus arise 'about the importance of reciprocity and the importance of sustaining the kinds of interpersonal relationships which generate these benefits'.

Filial obligations, or obligations of daughters and sons, arise so as 'not to frustrate legitimate expectations of those with whom one intimately co-operates to produce mutual benefits of fundamental importance'. To Mills the question is not so much 'must I?' as 'how can I not?' So the 'cycle of familial reciprocity' does not create 'debts' to be 'repaid', it affirms the importance of families as social units for the mutual benefit of all family members, as units that foster the sort of intimacy that does not make it difficult to accept moral obligations to family members. Asian cultures in particular have a strong sense of filial obligation. Beside filial obligations, familial reciprocity includes obligations between partners and between siblings. Admittedly, it is easier to fulfil these obligations where they have been mutually shared over the years. It is less easy to fulfil these responsibilities to relatives who have been miserly, stingy, rude, care only when it suits them, or who have largely ignored us until now when they need us.

Social obligations

To conclude, as Alan Wolfe, Professor of Sociology and writer on civil society, maintains, *moral obligation provides the girders for moral societies.* Girders provide firm frameworks for the construction of large objects. Societies with solid girders respect *individual rights* and *social responsibilities*: what *we have*, and what *we owe*. I have tried to show that intimate association in the family provides a solid groundwork for recognising unique individuality. Along with this recognition comes the mutual respect of others' rights, and the acceptance of the obligation to care for others. Indeed, this respect on which obligation is based is the respect that is integral to the minimal ethical code valid for all societies, and it is the precursor of a rights-regarding moral community.

This is a community that takes individual rights seriously, but that avoids individualism because it places rights alongside networks of social obligations. This accords tremendous value to human relationships, and to the way individuals in particular relationships interact to make the moral order viable. Moral obligations are not restricted to the intimate realm, but require us to come together in civil society, to accept the inevitability of disagreements, to discuss options, to be flexible and tolerant, to promote the well-being of others, and to be accountable for the way we live our everyday life as moral agents who are part of an interdependent social network.

The restoration of obligation as a positive social concept is necessary to reinstate important social bonds that individualism has broken apart. These social bonds are based on a realisation that we do owe our friends, our workmates, and our communities the attempt to promote social co-operation, and this enhances the quality of our social interaction. That is, co-operation with others means that we need to listen, to share, to debate, and to come to some acceptable decision—whether this concerns all agenda items for a staff meeting, the sale of pigs, the export of wool, the joint custody of children, or a ceasefire. The stronger our attachment, the stronger is our sense of obligation to the family, the group, the friend, the organisation, the institution, the work place, or the nation. Our connections to others means that we ask not just 'what can I get myself?' but 'what should I do for others?' In a context of *mutual obligation*, where those we associate with are also asking these questions, we can safely assume that our associates will facilitate our getting some of what we desire.

These types of obligations are pertinent at all sociopolitical levels. International politics increasingly seeks world co-operation to assist global concerns of ecology, sustainable economies, fair trade, and peace. Where these concerns are threatened, major world powers take with utmost seriousness their obligations to protect, to penalise, and to prevent. At a political level, federal, state, and local councils have different obligations to each other, and to their constituents, according to size, budget, capacity to legislate, and the varying needs of different communities. Economies have responsibilities to the planet to be ecologically holistic, to their workers to be fair, and to their competitors to negotiate reasonably. The Public or Civil Service has an intense obligation to uphold the welfare of citizens in issues of financial security, housing, education, health, and protection from violence. Where organisations accept obligations as a sign of commitment to attachments, social co-operation is likely to enhance the operation of an organisation—whether this organisation is a corporate body, an educational establishment, a charity, a church, a building construction company, a retail structure, a professional consortium, a sports league, an entertainment group, or a financial syndicate. Moral obligations are pertinent at every level of social association.

12

Building Small Democracies

'Tell me what kind of family you have and I'll tell you what kind of society you have'.

Frederic Le Play, nineteenth-century French social analyst

The relationship between family life and citizenship life is intimate; they influence each other. To have good societies we need to develop good families as the base unit of society. Let me reiterate the overall themes of this book in order to place this discussion in context. Families are changing. Some of these changes come as a result of social changes, but family structures themselves are changing, and altering social structures. On a global scale, many of these changes are associated with work for wages substituting family-based subsistence labour, along with economic modernisation and all that is attached to this, like improvements in communication, transport, media, education, increased awareness of lifestyle options, and changing social values.

One of the significant changes that has arisen from modern relationships between the family, market, and civil life, is the acceleration of individualism. Individualism ranks self-fulfilment over group fulfilment, and self-interest occurs at the expense of a strong sense of moral obligation to others. Individualism destroys meaningful family networks. I have maintained consistently that good societies need good families—good single-parent families, good nuclear families, good blended families, good indigenous families, good extended families and so on.

190

12 Building Small Democracies 191

To call something 'good' suggests a moral goodness involving the sorts of *virtues* that make us good persons, good families, and good communities. It also suggests a *purpose to the goodness*, that we are striving toward some aim, such as determining what is entailed in *being a good family*. I have suggested that the good of the family is its well-being, and this includes the well-being of individuals, the family, and the role of the family in the community. An important part of fostering this well-being is in instilling social, cultural, spiritual, and moral values, and in providing a strong sense of secure belonging—a connectedness to others that establishes the grounding for a moral obligation towards others in the community.

Good families foster strong moral character, an active notion that connects goodness, virtue, and practical wisdom. Virtues, as we now understand, are those dispositions of character that make a person good; they refer to the excellence of fulfilling our task, such as practising the qualities necessary to build good families. Knowing how to do this relies less on rigid moral rules than on a capacity to act with regard to human goods. This *practical wisdom* depends on *good habits and good judgements*; we learn to be moral by being moral. We learn to create good families by *being good families*. These are not slick clichés. I am reinforcing the point that becoming good families is an on-going, active notion. We owe it to ourselves, to our families, and to our communities to develop ourselves as active, responsible moral agents. This respect for agent selfhood is a respect for one's self and for others as persons of moral character.

Clearly this goal of creating good families is not being achieved everywhere. Families are under enormous economic, social, and emotional pressures. As Henryk Sokalski, Co-ordinator of the International Year of the Family (1994), outlines, 'too many human beings, lacking the care and support of others, are homeless, helpless, hungry, hostile, angry, misfit, misguided, mistreated, poor, illiterate, disenfranchised, drug or alcohol addicted, rootless, purposeless, abused or abusive'. The family is clearly implicated in these devastating personal situations. In this concluding chapter I ask three final questions.

- Why are good families very important?
- What are the connections between private and public life?
- How do good families create good citizens?

We are exploring how the quality of family life affects social outcomes and our sense of moral obligation to others.

Why are Good Families Important?

Good families are very important because they are the *basic unit of all societies*, whatever their cultural variance. Despite mammoth sociological changes, families continue to provide the framework for the material and emotional support and nurture for dependants, and the profound need for intimate companionship and security for adults. A further prime function of families is the transmission of cultural values, the values and symbols our cultures regard highly and which inform us what is of merit, of significance, of social importance, and what is a cultural virtue. Cultures vary enormously here. One culture might see large families as a sign of family prosperity and a security for parental old age. Another culture might measure wealth by material goods, calculating the cost of having children against this. Together with religious symbolism, cultural values give meaning to life. Cultural pluralism and secularism removes much of the shared basis to symbolic meaning. This loss creates an urgency for families to foster the enlightening and enriching aspects of living that provide us with a sense of significance, and which are important for people who are not religious, as well as those who are.

Given that the family is the basic unit of society, then societies need to support all families, not just those who appear destitute, dysfunctional, or divided. Prevention is always better than cure. We need to ensure that the basic necessities for family living are within the scope of people's options. For example, we criticise families who sell their daughters as prostitutes and their young sons as labourers, or disfigure their children to attract sympathy as beggars. But societies, particularly wealthier ones, also have an obligation to ensure that no family should ever have to do this, that there is adequate housing, health facilities, education, access to food and work, income security measures, child allowances, sickness benefits, and appropriate exemptions for necessities one cannot afford. The rise in number of street kids and homeless persons is a shocking indictment on social values. Families are a private and a public concern, thus the support of the family's well-being must be shared.

In the words of Don Edgar, sociologist and researcher on family studies, 'all families need support, not just needy families'. In examining the tendencies of the welfare state, Alan Tapper, historian and philosopher, notes an imbalance against families with children in favour of independent individuals, and against intact families in favour of families which break up. Understandably, sole parent families need additional assistance, particularly women-headed households who often experience a marked decline in living standards as a result of a separation or a divorce, and who frequently do not have the work experience or qualifications necessary to find the sort of work that would adequately support a household.

But family policies also need to affirm the *value of stable families* through legislation and family support services, like parent education, health education, access to books on parenting, play resources, the provision of emergency relief care, and family support services in local neighbourhoods. Policies need to support the undeniably social nature of our existence and the universal need for companionship and intimacy. In Tapper's words, 'political leaders might seek to restore the self-confidence of families with children, and might sponsor policies which give families real status in society'. This emphasis might also encourage governments to review the effect of their policies on all types of families.

Another practical way to acknowledge the value of families is for societies to recognise the real worth of unpaid caring roles, that *caring fulfils a crucial social function*. When families care responsibly for their family members, this certainly saves the state from spending public money. When the family does not fulfil its obligations to care for dependants, the very elderly, and the handicapped, substitutes need to be found. But it is precisely this preoccupation with economics that obscures the real social importance of care. The value of the place where we are nurtured and nurture others, where workers rest, are sustained, and regain energy for a productive contribution to the economy, is undervalued in a system where anything of value supposedly has its material price.

Good families are important because they:

- instil cultural, social, spiritual, and moral values
- support the social, emotional, and material needs of family members
- nurture and provide socially necessary care
- aim for the well-being of all family members
- provide a place of security, belonging, connectedness, and companionship
- foster a sense of moral obligations to others.

Good families really do matter.

Connections between Private and Public Life

Good families make a significant contribution to the *well-being of society*. The nature of the private–public and the family–social link is complex; it requires us to reconcile our autonomous individuality with our essential sociability. As I have repeated in this book, we are individual, social beings. Edgar captures this complexity well. 'It is the love relationship which preserves at least the elements of a more connected social ecology. At the same time, it is the private mores of the isolated family group which often prevent us from seeing our public place, from serving our civic obligations to others'. Why is this so?

Certainly as soon as public paid work became separate from the private household, new forms of family life emerged. In the bourgeois classes there was a master/mistress/servant division similar to the breadwinner/housewife separation that operated in many of the families that we were reared in. Now there are a range of economic options like single-headed households, the dual income family where there is still a prime breadwinner and a second person brings in some income, a dual career family with both partners pursuing a profession, and a dual domicile-separated family. Economic structural changes and familial structural changes impact on each other.

Family, work, and individualism

Accompanying these changes in family and work, is, as we have remarked, the growth of individualism. I have given many examples of ways in which western liberal individualist cultures concentrate on the individual, maintaining a separate identity, and being self-sufficient. This orientation influences the nature of marriage and committed partnerships in particular ways, in that it has become a context for the expression of individuality, of choice, personal preference, and mutual negotiations. In this milieu, children are not essential to family life; they are part of the emphasis on choice. While an emphasis on individuality allows us to express our choice, individualism often undermines the other-oriented values we have examined.

The women's movement has contributed significantly to the push for individual rights, fighting against the situation in which the whole family is seen to be represented by the household head, the property-owning male. Understandably, women have fought long and hard to be considered autonomous individuals in their own right, irrespective of their relation to a man. Furthermore, aware of the potentially devastating financial situations they can be left in if they separate from the man they have been dependent on, women are now wary of the pitfalls of economic dependency. Increasing numbers of women want career options, to be in control of their personal earnings, and where possible to share the economic and parenting responsibilities with their partners.

Many men are in an ambiguous situation. On the one hand they are relieved at the lessened burden that sole breadwinning induces. On the other hand, for many men, competition in the labour market, making money, and breadwinning is an intrinsic part of masculine identity, and it is this identity that is somehow threatened not only when a partner is contributing to economic provision, but when men are expected to participate in domestic chores and child-rearing tasks. The sheer economic pressures of surviving in economies where inflation, expensive housing, materialistic pressures, increasing costs related to children, and decreasing government expenditure on welfare services are the norm, will mean that in most two-parent families both parents will need to work for wages. Most single-parent families will be at a financial disadvantage.

Needs and wants differ. The endless self-seeking of individualism has two main implications for the relationship between work and family. First, work capitalises on the individualistic surge. Secondly, the self-sufficient individual devalues dependency, which as we have seen is an integral part of interdependency. First, as Edgar also argues, the self-seeking approach to life plays an important function for paid work. When there are individuals uncommitted to others, or individuals determined to succeed at all costs, work has a pool of mobile, competitive, interchangeable workers. As Edgar argues, 'if our work structures, our education and media systems, our role models both inside and outside the family are all reinforcing the legitimacy of a focus on self, then it is hardly surprising that there is a loss of altruism, of connectedness to our fellows, a rejection of our shared human obligations and need for one another'.

The second part of this loss is that when self-sufficiency is held up as a goal for all, dependency is stigmatised. Women do not like dependency on men. Young people, particularly the unemployed looking for work, do not want to be entirely dependent on their parents. The disabled do not like to be totally dependent on the able-bodied. But dependency is a central part of the human condition. It is one dimension that distinguishes us from the animals, we have the longest period of childhood dependency, effectively eighteen years.

Dependency highlights our vulnerability to others—we have to trust others, and rely on others as it is part of the need for social co-operation. In Edgar's words, dependency is 'one end of the continuum of interdependence, exchange, negotiation, conflict and power'. When we teach our children not only the importance of individual rights, fulfilment, and self-expression, but also the importance of sharing, of giving to others, of co-operation with others, of the delights of mutuality, and of the need to take seriously our responsibility to others, then we are educating them to see independence as part of the interdependency needed for good families and for good citizenship.

Society pays a high price for extreme individualism; it affects the cultural significance placed on connections to others, on interdependent networks, and on responsibilities and obligations assumed for the needs of others. Yet, despite the strength of individualistic tendencies, pro-family ideals remain evident. Children are still valued highly despite their enormous costs, as a source of great enrichment to life, and perhaps as a security for old age, which may be of an economic nature in some cultures, and may be expected to minimise extreme loneliness in all cultures. Marriage is still held in high regard, despite increasing numbers of cohabiting and de facto relationships. Divorce is not taken lightly and remarriages are common. Thus we are caught; we want intimacy and close companionship, yet we fight against interdependence in our individual assertion of self-sufficiency.

Parenting and work

These tensions are conspicuous as a result of the overlap between private family responsibilities and public work demands. For women with children in particular, who value child-rearing in a way men typically value money-making, there is a constant need to shuffle work and family responsibilities. No matter how tiring, or how demanding the day's paid work has been, the football boots have to be taken to the shoe repairer, the youngest taken to the doctor, medicines purchased, the oldest taken to and picked up from the gym, bread and milk bought, the dinner cooked, cleaning up supervised, a load of washing taken in and folded, another load done, homework supervised, a phone call to a sick parent made, and the school newsletters read. What people without children do not realise is that this is not an abnormally busy day, this is a typical day in the life of a family with working parent(s), and children. It is because of these continuous demands that women often prefer part-time work.

The combination of work and family responsibilities creates a series of potential difficulties that include the psychological demands of juggling and often having to rank contrasting commitments, shift work, tiredness, fatigue, exhaustion, care of sick children and ageing parents, erratic concentration at work, lateness, and early leaving. What employers must realise is that childcare and care of dependants is not a private women's issue. It is a social issue and a long-term necessity to economic productivity. The combination of work and family responsibilities is also a concern for men. Most young children have two living biological parents, and many children now have additional social, adopted, or step-parents. All parents must accept responsibility for their children.

It is essential for good societies to recognise that 'being a parent' and meeting familial obligations should not penalise anyone in terms of job security, seniority, or promotion. Parents need access to maternity and paternity leave, to quality childcare of a private, public, or community nature, either at work, near work, or near home, provision of after-school care, time off for sick children and close relatives, days off for meeting urgent family needs and emergencies, and flexible work schedules. These provisions are not private luxuries; contented employees with satisfactory domestic lives boost economic efficiency. We need to continue working out sensitive responses to the intricate connections between family and work life.

Good Families, Good Citizens

Individualism is at odds with a life of virtue. *Being virtuous* is being part of sustaining worthwhile traditions of morality. That is, *being a good person* is tantamount to *being a good citizen*, someone concerned with relationships with others, in both private and public settings. To characterise a good person as a good citizen is to draw close links between all aspects of our lives. This is because *citizenship*, as I am using it, refers to the *participation in common projects* which are valued by the community in which the citizen resides. It is a direct involvement in the processes through which people associate together. In this final section I want to argue three concluding points:

12 Building Small Democracies

- Society is influenced by the character of its citizens;
- Social bonds require a series of common purposes;
- Virtues are the habits needed to sustain civic solidarity.

We need to delve further into the nature of how our social individuality is constituted, how common purposes emerge, and how a civic solidarity can cement a sense of belonging.

1 Social individuality

Modern individualism says 'I am what I choose to be'. In a positive sense, this is the freedom of self-expressive individuality outlined in Chapter 3. Yet frequently this expression goes to extreme lengths where the modern individual lives only for the moment, for self-satisfaction, excitement, and fulfilment of self-interest. And this individual orientation is far removed from the Athenian virtues on which I have based much of this book's argument. Alasdair MacIntyre, political theorist, suggests that we have two major things to learn from an ancient society where the self was never considered as a detached being. The first factor is that all morality is 'tied to the socially local and particular'. It is not *ad hoc*, abstract, reduced to self-preference, or divorced from our concrete situations. Secondly, and because of this first factor, 'there is no way to possess the virtues except as part of a tradition in which we inherit them'. The choices we make, the type of people we are, the way we live our lives, and relate to others, *contextualises morality*.

Virtues are not separate from our everyday lives; they are part of our embodied selfhood. Our self identity, our social identity, our historical identity, and our moral identity coincide in concrete contexts, sometimes uncomfortably, sometimes conflictually, and sometimes harmoniously, but nevertheless, all contributing to our life's narrative. To extend MacIntyre's argument, we approach our life's circumstances as bearers of particular identities, as daughters, sons, wives, husbands, sisters, brothers, as citizens of this cultural group, this community, this nation, and these roles provide our moral starting point. That is, we draw extensively on our relationships and concrete practical situations before making important choices.

If I know my father is sentimental, I will make sure I am not away for his birthday. If I know my sister grieves the death of her daughter, I will be sensitive to her as my own daughter graduates, becomes a journalist, and has her own daughter.

Sometimes these socially constructed roles seem inappropriate. They may cramp our styles. As *active moral agents* we are not bound to accept the moral limitations of our particular situations but, in questioning, we challenge our constraints, we keep searching for the good, we debate suggestions about good conduct with others, and we confirm the contextual nature of morality. As MacIntyre puts it, the freedom of choice of values on which modernity prides itself is a 'freedom of ghosts' for ancient societies. We do not make our moral decisions as shadowy ghosts, we make them in everyday living contexts, with ordinary everyday relationships. 'To characterise a good person is in crucial part to characterise the relationship in which such a person stands to others.' As I defined it in the Introduction, *morality* is concerned with our *attentive responsiveness to others*.

To reiterate, in referring back to ancient virtues, I am not advocating an unrealistic, romantic return to a past that was perfect. Indeed, these ancient societies excluded women and slaves from full participation. Rather, I consider it important to draw on a way of understanding the self as intricately connected with traditions that provide a moral grounding, and then to translate this understanding into cultures moving into the twenty-first century. The adaptation of this understanding requires expansive notions of selfhood, what Nancy Rosenblum, political theorist, calls 'thick selves', that is, selves that correspond to the 'thick' notion of the good outlined in Chapter 1.

As we have observed, this notion of self considers individuality and commonality, the place of the individual in groups like families, local communities, social organisations, cultures, and nations as an integral part of what it means to be an individual. This *belonging binds people*, it contextualises morality, and makes it relevant. What is good for an individual, for families, and for citizens is not merely given by laws, philosophers, or gods. Rather, these 'goods', as political theorist Michael Walzer expresses it, 'are themselves socially constituted by shared experiences, communal meanings, and traditions of self-understanding that evolve through history'. In order to ascertain more clearly what is involved in these 'goods' we need continual public debate about common purposes.

2 Common purposes

The point about searching for common purposes is not to impose a unitary, universal set of values, not to constrain free choice, nor to assume a one-dimensional superiority of views. Rather, it is about searching for a deeper understanding of what groups share in common and, from this understanding, working out what makes individuals in these groups flourish. Single mothers in poverty, indigenous people deprived of land rights, refugees, raped women, children who do not know their natural parents, violent abusive men, homeless youth, peasant farmers, illiterate outworkers, and young brides of arranged marriages—all these groups have common interests. All sorts of factors keep people apart.

To extend the examples above, marginalisation through poverty, ignorance of options, displacement, fear, uncertainty, arrogance, concern with mere survival, dominating restrictiveness, and self-interest prevent groups from meeting together to discuss shared common interests. There are mutual benefits in sharing that include personal interests and group interests. What arises from the recognition of *common interests in the common good* is a collective effort to sustain *social morality*.

As MacIntyre reminds us, what education in the virtues teaches is that 'my good as a person is the good of others with whom I am bound up in human community'. A shared recognition of the pursuit of the good is a sharing which is primary to any meaningful notion of community. This does not require total agreement on the good, but the *shared pursuit* in itself is important. The pursuit brings people together in co-operation in order to search for ways to satisfy various goals. Certainly opposition and debate is essential to the democratic process. But for example, in politics, if rival parties only emphasise their differences, impasses continually occur. When parties recognise that they share common aims—a desire for peace, good employment prospects, health services, and so forth, then there is a basis for recognising common goals, connections, and joint purposes.

This might sound like an oversimplification, but to reiterate, modernity holds an enormous range of ideas on what is good for humans—a pluralism of moral values is a sociological realism. My point is that there are moral ways to cope with plural views without resorting to moral relativism. Relativism suggests that there are no universal moral principles, and that there can be no reconciliation of differences of morality, so everything is permissible. Always emphasising differences means that we lose sight of the possibility of shared purposes.

Mutual respect is a key virtue at the core of these sorts of shared moral deliberations of citizens. Amy Gutmann and Dennis Thompson, political theorists, express this clearly. 'Like toleration, mutual respect is a form of agreeing to disagree. But mutual respect demands more than toleration. It requires a favourable attitude toward, and constructive interaction with, the persons with whom one disagrees.' These writers see mutual respect as a feature of individuals who are morally committed to determining legitimate common interests, discerning differences between respectable differences of opinion, and being open to modifying or changing their own views. This is very different from the relativism mentioned above. Citizens must have *principled procedures to disagree* so, to draw on examples I have used in other chapters, citizens might disallow choices that hurt others, that undermine human dignity, and that do not appear to be genuinely caring.

Choices need coherent defences. As I have frequently argued, practical reasoning involves deliberation over what are conflicting views, and requires give and take between general principles that seem to apply to everyone and the concrete particularity of individual situations which is needed in order to make a moral choice. I am stressing that when common purposes are involved, our practical task is to discover common ground to reconcile or to cope with differences, and *dialogue and debate* is crucial to keep the *open nature of morality* vibrant. Total agreement is rarely possible, thus it is our mutual respect for others and our practical judgement which informs us what morality requires of us.

3 Civic solidarity

To bring together our social individuality and our search for common purposes we need a strong notion of civic solidarity, a restoration of an *intense sense of social bonds, a deep-rooted notion of community*, and a *fervent sense of moral obligation to others*. I have repeatedly maintained that we realise ourselves as individuals only through being intrinsically tied to others. Mutual instrumental ties of contract, whether economic or sexual, cannot alone bond individuals together. So what can? What I am advocating is *human interdependence* as the basis for familial, social, and civic interaction. We need each other.

What we require are *social ethics*, where citizenship is fulfilled by members advancing goals that have been debated rigorously and seem to aim at the good of the society. The concrete needs we share are not private goals, but the means toward *social goals* like our need for affective bonds, love, intimacy, companionship, friendship, and co-operation between political organisations and nations. How do we start developing a social ethic that builds civic solidarity? Quite simply by working through the personal implications of some of the suggestions in this book, that:

- good families are important and worth striving toward;
- our public and private lives are interrelated and should be ethical;
- good citizenship is dependent on the fostering of good families.

An ideal of communities where citizens realise some solidarity does not deny differences between citizens. Rather, it minimises the self-interested competitiveness of separate, self-contained persons who continually push their individual differences in an antagonistic way. Appreciating the benefits of differences provides the strength of diversity. An emphasis on community can attend to the particularity of shared and differing needs in a way individualism cannot. In taking civic solidarity seriously, we need to take into account:

- what we share with each other, and how we differ from each other

- our personal autonomy, and the need for intimacy
- our individuality and the need for communal solidarity.

What we seek is:
- personal freedom and self-realisation
- security and togetherness
- a sense of autonomy and a sense of attachment.

Communal solidarity can support both strong individual and strong collective sentiment when there is a personal commitment and a collective responsibility toward ensuring that all have an equitable opportunity to pursue self-development within social settings.

Bonds of solidarity rely on our *social interaction*, our sense of belonging and our commitment to citizenship. As families, social groups, communities, and citizens, we have a shared fate, we must co-operate with each other. This sharing is valuable; it tightens the bonds and it encourages us to think through the differences between 'I' and 'we', and the relationship between individuality and community. It is in these social contexts where the moral virtues discussed in this book actually achieve a recognisable form, where the sharing in common unites people in an *ethic of citizenship*. This ethic strives to benefit the community as a whole by encouraging good families, educational reform, leisure groups, cultural enrichment for the economically deprived, active parishes, specific support groups, or an economic restructuring that takes into account people's real needs.

Václav Havel, President of Czechoslovakia in 1992, writes of political life as a service to others. The roots of this service 'are moral because it is a responsibility, expressed through action, to and for the whole'. Our world is becoming increasingly interdependent in trade, ecology, knowledge, communication, and peace. To be globally successful, 'there is only one way to strive for decency, reason, responsibility, sincerity, civility and tolerance: and that is decently, reasonably, responsibly, sincerely, civilly, and tolerantly'. This is an idea of politics that takes private and public conscience seriously; it is a political citizenship as the practice of morality.

It is also the political equivalent of my oft-repeated phrase, 'the only way to create good families is by *being* good families'.

My aim in this book has been to set the framework in which a *moral community* of various types of families can emerge. This is not a revamped version of 'old families', nor the pro-family movement of the new right which relocates women as sole carers; not only as an answer to male unemployment, but also to the state's welfare bill. Rather, it is a community of families who seek the mutual growth of all its family members, a growth that sees individuals affirming themselves through collective identification, commitment, and responsibility.

The links between family and social citizenship are intimate. As Henryk Sokalski puts it, 'peace in the family holds the promise of peace in society generally. The family which treats its individuals with mutual respect, empathy and kindness is an example to the community and greater society'. It is like trying to build 'the smallest democracy at the heart of society'. To do this means building families where the range of needs are met, where our differences are accepted, and our rights are respected. This provides a platform from which we can all make a meaningful contribution to a good life in the home, the community, and the greater society. To return to the quote at the start of this chapter, the quality of family life is a reflection of the moral depth of the society. Good families matter. The only way to create good families is by being good families.

Bibliography

Aristotle, *The Basic Works of Aristotle*, (ed.) R. McKeon. Random House, New York, 1941.

Baier, Annette, 'Trust and Antitrust', *Ethics*, vol. 96, 1986, pp. 231–60.

Bailey-Harris, Rebecca, *Defining the Family for the Twenty-First Century*, Inaugural Lecture, Foundation Professor of Law, Flinders University of South Australia, 6 March 1992.

Benjamin, Jessica, *The Bonds of Love: psychoanalysis, feminism, and the problem of domination*. Virago, London, 1988.

Bird, Gloria, and Melville, Keith, *Families and Intimate Relationships*. McGraw-Hill, New York, 1994.

Bloom, Allan, *The Closing of the American Mind*. Simon & Schuster, New York, 1987.

Blum, Lawrence, 'Iris Murdoch and the Domain of the Moral', *Philosophical Studies*, vol. 50, 1986, pp. 343–67.

Card, Claudia, 'Caring and Evil', *Hypatia*, vol. 5, no. 1, 1990, pp. 101–8.

—— (ed.), *Feminist Ethics*. University Press of Kansas, Kansas, 1991, esp. 'Whom Can Women Trust?', pp. 233–45.

Duck, Steve, *Human Relationships: an introduction to social psychology*. Sage Publishers, London 1986.

Edgar, Don, 'Conceptualising Family Life and Family Policies', *Family Matters*, no. 32, 1992, pp. 28–37.

Field, D. M., *Greek and Roman Mythology*. Hamlyn, London, 1977.

Foot, Philippa, *Virtues and Vices: and other essays in moral philosophy*. Basil Blackwell, Oxford, 1978.

Genovese, Elizabeth Fox, *Feminism Without Illusions: a critique of individualism*. University of North Carolina Press, Chapel Hill, 1991.

Gilligan, Carol, *In a Different Voice: psychological theory and women's development*. Harvard University Press, Cambridge, Mass., 1983.
────── 'Moral Orientation and Moral Development', in E. Feder Kittay and D. T. Meyers (eds), *Women and Moral Theory*. Rowman & Littlefield, New Jersey, 1987, pp. 19–36.
Gould, Carol (ed.), *Beyond Domination: new perspectives on women and philosophy*. Rowman & Allanheld, New Jersey, 1984.
Gutmann, Amy, and Thompson, Dennis, 'Moral Conflict and Political Consensus', in R. B. Douglass et al. (eds), *Liberalism and the Good*. Routledge, New York, 1990.
Habermas, Jürgen, *Communication and the Evolution of Society*, trans. T. McCarthy. Heinemann, London, 1979.
Havel, Václav, 'Paradise Lost', *New York Review*, 9 April 1992, pp. 6–7.
Held, Virginia, *Rights and Goods: justifying social action*. Free Press, New York, 1984.
────── 'Feminist Transformations of Moral Theory', *Philosophy and Phenomenological Research*, vol. 50 Supplement, 1990, pp. 321–44.
Ibsen, Henrik, *Plays*, trans. P. Watts. Penguin, Harmondsworth, 1973.
Ignatieff, Michael, *The Needs of Strangers*. Chatto & Windus, London, 1984.
Jordan, Bill, *The Common Good: citizenship, morality and self-interest*. Basil Blackwell, Oxford, 1989.
MacIntyre, Alasdair, *After Virtue: a study in moral theory*. Duckworth, London, 1982.
────── 'The Privatization of Good: an inaugural lecture', *Review of Politics*, no. 52, 1990, pp. 344–61.
Mills, Claudia (ed.), *Value and Public Policy*. Harcourt Brace Jovanovich, New York, 1992.
Murdoch, Iris, *The Sovereignty of Good*. Routledge & Kegan Paul, London, 1970.
Nussbaum, Martha, 'Human Functioning & Social Justice: in defense of Aristotelian essentialism', *Political Theory*, vol. 20, no. 2, 1992, pp. 202–46.
Plato, *Works*. Heinemann, London, 1955.
Porter, Elisabeth, *Women and Moral Identity*. Allen & Unwin, Sydney, 1991.

Rawls, John, *A Theory of Justice.* Oxford University Press, Oxford, 1971.
Rice, F. Philip, *Intimate Relationships, Marriages, and Families.* Mayfield Publishing Company, California, 1993.
Rosenblum, Nancy (ed.), *Liberalism and the Moral Life.* Harvard University Press, Cambridge, Mass., 1989.
Rubin, Lillian, *Just Friends: the role of friendship in our lives.* Harper & Row, New York, 1985.
Ruddick, Sara, *Maternal Thinking: toward a politics of peace.* Beacon Press, Boston, 1989.
Sandel, Michael, 'The Procedural Republic and the Unencumbered Self', in T. B. Strong (ed.), *The Self and the Political Order.* Blackwell, Oxford, 1992.
Scanzoni, John, *Shaping Tomorrow's Family: theory and policy for the twenty-first century.* Sage, Beverly Hills, 1983.
Shakespeare, W. *Complete Works of Shakespeare.* Co-operative Publications Society, New York, 1885.
Sokalski, Henryk, 'Building the Smallest Democracy at the Heart of Society', *Ita,* February 1993, pp. 56–7.
Tapper, Alan, *The Family in the Welfare State.* Allen & Unwin, Sydney, 1990.
Taylor, Charles, 'Irreducibly Social Goods', in G. Brennan and C. Walsh (eds), *Rationality, Individualism and Public Policy.* Centre for Research on Federal Financial Relations, Canberra, 1990.
―――― *Multiculturalism and the 'Politics of Recognition'*, with commentary by A. Gutmann (ed.). Princeton University Press, Princeton, New Jersey, 1992.
Tillich, Paul, *Morality and Beyond.* Routledge & Kegan Paul, London, 1964.
Walzer, Michael, *Spheres of Justice: a defence of pluralism and equality.* Basil Blackwell, Oxford, 1983.
―――― 'The Communitarian Critique of Liberalism', *Political Theory,* vol. 18, no. 1, 1990, pp. 6-23.
Wolfe, Alan, *Whose Keeper? Social Sciences and Moral Obligations.* University of California Press, Berkeley, 1989.

Index

affection, 15, 39, 44–5, 51, 100, 106, 112, 120–5, 129–31, 133–7, 139, 140–1, 148, 150–3, 179, 186

care, 7, 12, 15, 23, 26–7, 36, 39–40, 45, 51, 63, 73, 77, 80–1, 83, 86, 90–2, 97, 113, 115, 119–23, 125–31, 133–5, 142–3, 144–6, 150, 160, 165, 178, 182, 186–7, 191, 193–4, 198, 205

character, 16–19, 27–31, 37, 41–2, 55, 79, 81, 89, 103, 106, 138, 152, 168, 180, 191, 199

childcare, 45, 95, 111, 127–8, 136, 198

citizenship, 5, 7–8, 16, 21–2, 24, 28, 41, 60, 62, 70, 80, 93, 97, 134, 173, 176–7, 188, 190, 192, 197–200, 202, 203–5

commitment, 8, 12, 15, 20, 38–9, 71–2, 75–7, 79–82, 93, 106, 131, 135, 138, 143, 153–5, 184–6, 188, 198, 204–5

communication, 6, 44, 69, 130, 133, 149, 166, 190

commonality, 3, 5, 20–2, 32, 56, 133, 139, 141, 143–6, 148, 155, 179–81, 198–204

compassion, 32, 39, 112–6, 119, 128, 142, 179, 181

diversity, 20–3, 46, 69, 78, 203

domestic duties, 2, 13, 45, 52, 77, 111, 148, 170, 196, 198

domination, 142, 157, 160–1, 163–4, 166–9

elderly, 3, 52, 68, 96, 124, 135, 137, 193

equality, 21, 62, 68, 146, 152, 166, 170

ethics, contextualised, 16, 18–19, 22–4, 27–8, 32, 34–5, 37, 39, 59, 66, 71, 75, 81, 89, 92–6, 103–7, 109–110, 114–16, 118–19, 135, 152–4, 162, 166, 168–71, 179–80, 182, 188, 195, 199–200, 204

faithfulness, 38, 71–3, 76–7, 79, 81–2, 154, 186

family, definitions of, 9–10, 12–13

femininity, 44, 61–2, 127, 135, 160

finances, 3, 14, 52–3, 97, 162

flexibility, 37–8, 60, 64–9, 88, 103, 166

forgiveness, 39, 51, 94, 98–102, 104–6, 114–16, 118, 142, 182–3

friendship, 15–16, 23, 26, 35–6, 38–40, 42, 44–5, 47–9, 57, 66, 76, 88, 90, 97, 116, 138–9, 141, 143–55, 157, 169–70, 174, 186, 188, 203

gender differentiation, 11, 13, 43–6, 63, 112, 123, 125, 134, 148, 163–5, 170

goodness, 5, 9, 16–25, 29–35, 37–9, 50, 52, 54, 72, 107, 110–11, 137, 140–1, 146, 164, 176, 178, 185, 191, 200–1, 203

hurt, 1, 7, 39, 42, 48, 57–8, 63, 74, 83, 92, 94, 98–9, 105–6, 108, 115–16, 118, 124, 157, 169, 179, 182, 202

honesty, 38, 83–5, 87–9, 92–3, 95–7

209

Index

inclusion, 63–4, 128, 179
individualism, 13–15, 32, 40, 72, 74, 109, 121, 156, 172, 175, 178, 187–8, 190, 195–6, 197–9, 203
individuality, 14, 21, 24–5, 37, 40, 42, 46–9, 52, 54–5, 58, 94, 128, 141, 149, 156, 161, 170–2, 174, 179–80, 187, 194–5, 199–200, 203–4
interdependence, 8, 40, 42, 51, 128, 156–7, 159–61, 166, 169–71, 186, 196–7, 203
intimacy, 9, 12, 15, 21, 39, 51, 120–2, 131–3, 135, 143, 152, 154, 186–7, 193, 197, 203

justice, 8, 17, 21, 31, 39, 62, 98–9, 101, 106–19, 166, 172, 175

leisure, 45, 52–3, 62, 76–7, 113, 149, 175, 204
love, 26, 39, 51, 74, 78, 80, 87, 90, 110–11, 120–2, 124, 130, 132–3, 137–8, 139–44, 146–55, 160, 163, 169, 194, 203
loyalty, 38, 51, 71–3, 76–82, 84, 119, 150, 155, 186

masculinity, 13, 43–4, 60–2, 111, 123, 126, 152, 163, 169
mercy, 39, 51, 98–9, 112–16, 118–19
mistakes, 33, 37, 39, 56, 58, 90, 98–100, 113, 116, 129–30, 180, 183–4

negotiation, 37–8, 60, 66–70, 133, 186, 188
nuclear family, 9, 11–13, 24, 45, 190
nurturance, 12, 14, 27, 43–5, 91, 128, 135, 148, 152, 169–70, 192, 194

obligation, 8, 10, 14–15, 40, 51, 112, 115, 170, 173, 180–94, 196, 198, 203

partners, 8, 10–11, 13, 23, 26, 38–9, 51, 53, 56, 58, 64–5, 67, 72–6, 79, 95, 100–1, 105–6, 111, 117, 120–2, 132–5, 138–9, 141–2, 144–52, 154, 159, 162–3, 165–7, 179, 182, 185–7, 195
power, 15, 61–2, 68, 100, 111, 115, 127, 136, 140, 147, 157, 161, 163–9, 171, 176, 196
public, life, 4, 7–8, 19, 41, 59–62, 69–70, 75, 80–1, 84, 89, 93, 96–7, 99–100, 107, 110, 114, 116, 118, 120, 134–6, 153, 162–3, 170–1, 183, 186, 188, 192–4, 197–8, 201, 203–4
punishment, 39, 109, 118, 165

reciprocity, 6, 40
reliability, 38, 51, 71–2, 78–9, 81–2, 89, 186
respect, 6, 22–3, 37–8, 40, 55–6, 58–9, 80, 99, 104, 106, 112, 114, 141, 149, 151–2, 154, 156–7, 159, 171, 173, 176, 181, 183–4, 186–7, 191, 202, 205
responsibilities, 3, 12, 35, 45, 54, 59, 96, 115, 126, 128, 135, 155, 159, 161, 176, 180, 182, 197–8, 204–5
rights, 10, 14, 20–2, 40, 72, 106–7, 109–12, 114–17, 124, 126, 128, 134, 163–4, 172–80, 182, 186–7, 195–6, 201, 205

sex, 9–10, 26, 36, 38, 44, 49, 57, 63, 73–6, 79, 84, 117, 122–3, 129, 134, 140–1, 143, 145, 148–9, 154, 203
sexual abuse and control, 56, 91, 95, 111, 120–1, 137, 156, 159–64, 175, 182
siblings, 1–2, 11, 26, 38, 40, 63, 65, 68, 138, 144, 146–7, 150–1, 173–4, 176, 185, 187
single parents, 3, 11, 45–6, 53, 67, 78, 86, 91, 94, 100, 111, 113, 117, 124, 127, 134, 143, 145, 178, 190, 194, 196, 201
socialisation, 10, 12, 24–5, 44, 158, 160, 164
special ties, 2, 6, 9, 11–12, 15, 27, 51, 58, 91, 179, 185, 203

touch, 39, 50, 77, 121, 123–4, 135, 141
trust, 7, 18, 31, 34, 38–9, 51, 76, 79, 83–5, 89–97, 105, 142, 152, 154, 186, 196
truthfulness, 17, 22, 35, 38, 51, 83–90, 92–97, 146, 186

virtues, 8, 17–18, 24, 28–9, 31–5, 37–9, 41–2, 50, 55–6, 71–2, 76, 79–80, 82–4, 89, 92, 97–9, 103, 105–7, 113–16, 118–19, 122, 135, 139, 155–6, 183, 186, 191–2, 198–204

well-being, 7, 24, 27–8, 33, 41, 48, 55, 58, 60, 68, 73, 84, 98, 115, 129, 137, 142, 145–6, 152, 156, 177, 191, 193–4
wisdom, 28–9, 33–7, 41, 56, 65, 69, 84, 88, 103, 164, 191